A HANDBOOK ON INCULTURATION

Peter Schineller, S.J.

Paulist Press

New York · Mahwah

Library of Congress Cataloging-in-Publication Data

Schineller, Peter.
    A handbook on inculturation/Peter Schineller.
        p. cm.
    Includes bibliographical references.
    ISBN 0-8091-3124-2
    1. Christianity and culture. I. Title.
    BR115.C8S275   1990
    261—dc20   89-22969
                                                                      CIP

Published by Paulist Press
997 Macarthur Boulevard
Mahwah, NJ 07430

Printed and bound in the
United States of America

Contents

Introduction

In many churches in Zaire, Africa, there is a special form of the eucharistic liturgy commonly known as the Zaire rite mass. It begins with a procession of the whole community, many dressed in traditional clothing. There is traditional dancing as the gifts are brought forward. Many of the prayers of the mass are structured so as to call forth animated, continuous response from the participants. The entire joyful celebration may take as long as three hours. In the United States in November 1987, the bishops issued a lengthy pastoral letter entitled "Economic Justice for All" which followed their letters on peace and on Hispanic ministry.[1] In the library at the Catholic Institute of West Africa, in Port Harcourt, Nigeria, a young Nigerian priest conducts research into the traditional belief of the Igbo people in respect for ancestors; he seeks to relate this belief to Catholic belief in the communion of saints and to the church as the body of Christ.

All these incidents are examples of inculturation. They represent the efforts of Christians in particular places to understand and celebrate their Christian faith in a way peculiar to that situation or context. While sharing in the one, holy, catholic, and apostolic church, they are searching for the particular way in which this faith must be lived in their situation. Instead of a totally monolithic or uniform Catholic or Christian church, the catholicity of the church consists in the richness of its two thousand year tradition, a tradition extended not only in time but also in space.[2] We cherish with Vatican II the eastern Catholic churches with their own liturgical rites, their own canon law, their own rich heritage of spirituality. We look to Latin America for new insight into the gospel of God's love for the poor and the gospel challenge to liberation. And we look to Africa for a Christ yet to be discovered, a Christ who in the members of his body is himself African, in the words of Pope John Paul II.[3]

What is this phenomenon of inculturation, one that has always been present but is now emphasized in a new way as we expand our horizons and learn more about the world church? Where does inculturation come into play—only in Africa and Asia, or also in Europe and North America? And, most difficult of all, how does one begin to carry out the process of inculturation? These are questions that I wish to address in this introductory handbook on the vast challenge of inculturation.

In outline, I will first discuss what inculturation is and why inculturation is so important today. Then I will present briefly some key moments in the history of the Christian church that are significant for inculturation. Next I will explore the theological bases for inculturation and the important question of the method for carrying out the process. In the last chapters before the conclusion I will give examples of the beginnings of the process of inculturation in Africa and in the United States, and will examine liberation theology in Latin America as a contemporary example of inculturation.

Despite the significance of inculturation, surprisingly enough it is difficult to find an overview of it in one book. The number of both essays on inculturation and books describing certain aspects or examples is steadily increasing, but one searches in vain for a book on a basic, introductory level.[4]

My hope is that this book will provide some encouragement and guidance for ministers of the gospel in the first world as well as the third world. When he was superior general of the Society of Jesus, Pedro Arrupe referred to all ministers of the gospel as "agents of inculturation." Wherever the gospel is lived, wherever it is preached, we have the obligation to search continually for ways in which that good news can be more deeply lived, celebrated, and shared. This process is none other than the process of inculturation.

1. The What and Why of Inculturation

The Christian church finds itself immersed in the sweep of human history, affected by its problems and possibilities, by the victories and defeats of every age and culture. Inevitably the church moves through different phases in each of which a different aspect of the good news of Jesus Christ is emphasized. At the time of Vatican II, *aggiornamento* and *dialogue* were crucial terms used to designate the adaptation and interaction between church and world, between the Catholic Church and other Christian communities, and between Christianity and other religious traditions. With Pope Paul VI, the term *evangelization* emerged to describe the perennial mission of the church in sharing the good news. We pass through discussions of the *death of God* and the *secular city*. Whereas in Europe the topic has been political theology, in Latin America it remains the *theology of liberation*. The indispensable role of the *laity* in the mission of the church has received new emphasis since Vatican II. *Catechesis* is highlighted at international and national synods and conferences of bishops. *Solidarity* is a term that is often used by Pope John Paul II in his encyclicals and his addresses delivered during pastoral visits to various parts of the world. The list of key themes and current topics could go on.

The term that I will focus on has also emerged and at times been overused, namely, inculturation. What does this term refer to, and why has it emerged, what challenge does it present to the Christian church today, and how is it to be carried out? These are some of the questions I hope to answer.

5

Because the term is comparatively new and points to a complex reality or process, it is best to begin with a preliminary working definition or description of inculturation such as the following:

> Inculturation is the incarnation of Christian life and of the Christian message in a particular cultural context, in such a way that this experience not only finds expression through elements proper to the culture in question, but becomes a principle that animates, directs and unifies the culture, transforming and remaking it so as to bring about "a new creation."[1]

Inculturation, as this description suggests, ultimately goes back to the incarnation of Jesus Christ. "The Word became flesh and dwelt among us" (Jn 1:14). Jesus proclaimed the good news of the kingdom, and called apostles and disciples to continue that work after his own death and resurrection. "Go therefore and make disciples of all nations, baptizing them in the name of the Father, and of the Son, and of the Holy Spirit" (Mt 28:19). For almost two thousand years, the church has attempted to carry out this missionary mandate to share the good news throughout the world.

But why is there particular emphasis on inculturation in this day and age? Two reasons come to mind. First, I think it is because today more than ever we are in an age of mission, with tremendous challenge to and activity on the part of the church. Second, we are in an age of global awareness, which includes the awareness of cultural diversity. This diversity or pluralism is seen both within one nation, such as the United States, and when comparing one nation with another. Education, literature, and the mass media make us more aware than ever of the rich and basic differences between cultures. The United States is not the same as an African village, nor is one African village in Nigeria the same as one in Kenya, nor even are two Nigerian villages totally the same. Cultural anthropologists are trained experts on cultural differences, but everyone is at least aware of these differences. In the United States we realize that the Hispanic community differs from the black community as well as from the suburban middle class community. The church in Boston is not exactly the same as the church in Santa Fe. Christians of Italian heritage have different traditions and sensibilities than Christians of German or Korean background.

All of this, we now see, is of great import for the proclamation and living out of the gospel. The young child has different questions, different outlooks and needs, from those of the aging. We know that men view life and its problems and possibilities differently than women do.[2] And yet it is to this pluralistic world that the gospel must be preached. Hence the need for reflection on how this can be done in particular situations, the need for inculturation.

Jesus Christ, for example, *the* model of incarnation and inculturation, became incarnated in one particular time and place. Even there he spoke differently to his own apostles than he did to the scribes and Pharisees, differently to the Samaritan woman than to Peter. He could be stern or gentle. He knew when to speak and when to be silent. He was sensitive to the generosity of the widow at the temple, and to the need for affection on the part of the children who sought his blessing. His entire life and ministry remain the central paradigm for uncovering and inculturating gospel values of the kingdom into particular contexts.

In the speeches of Peter in the Acts of the Apostles, and very clearly in the speeches and letters of Paul, we see this process of inculturation continuing. One good example is the speech of Paul in Athens at the Areopagus (Acts 17). Here Paul relates his perception of the good news of Jesus Christ, present and risen, to the Greek philosophies and religion of his day. As we will see later, Paul's missionary activity to the Gentiles was an especially difficult test case in inculturation for the early Christian community—a case of great significance for the process of inculturation today. His way of writing letters to address particular pastoral problems and opportunities in the various churches he had established again illuminates the path that inculturation should take today.

In addition to the letters of Paul, the existence of the four gospels indicates the absolute necessity of inculturation. The story of Jesus is multifaceted, and the communities to whom the good news was preached were also diverse. Some were Jewish Christians and others were Gentiles; some were struggling under persecution while others were flourishing and expanding. Under the inspiration of the Spirit and through the creative efforts of the first Christians, the story of Jesus is presented in the gospels of Matthew, Mark, Luke, and John. Each of them provides both a model for inculturation and also a message to be inculturated, the good news of God's love in Jesus Christ. And each of them presents this good news in its own particular creative, inspired way.

That process must continue today. To show how the modern church regards this challenge, I quote from a speech of Pope John Paul II to African bishops:

> By respecting, preserving, and fostering the particular values and richness of your people's cultural heritage, you will be in a better position to lead

them to a better understanding of the mystery of Christ, which is to be lived in the noble, concrete, and daily experience of African life. . . . It is a question of bringing Christ into the very center of African life, and lifting up all African life to Christ. Thus not only is Christianity relevant to Africa, but Christ in the members of his body is himself African.[3]

To gain some perspective on the question of inculturation, on why it has emerged as a new imperative for the church today, let us examine briefly a now classic essay of Karl Rahner interpreting the meaning of the Second Vatican Council.[4] Rahner explains that there have been three major epochs, or eras, in church history.

In the first epoch the gospel was spread through the preaching of Jesus to his Jewish audience. This process was continued after his death and resurrection by the disciples and apostles as they lived among, and shared their faith with, the Jewish community. The result was Jewish Christianity, in which Christians retained many of the Jewish ways of praying, the Jewish law of circumcision, and some of the dietary laws.

The second era opened with the conversion of Paul and his subsequent mission to the Gentiles. Paul, born a Jew, after his conversion took the gospel message of Jesus to the Gentiles or non-Jews. Since their culture and religion was very different from Jewish culture and religion, Paul began to adapt the gospel to the new audience. The result was a Gentile form of Christianity, one that did not demand circumcision of its followers and that engaged in dialogue with Greek and Roman philosophy. According to Rahner, this is the basic form of Christianity that has lasted for almost two thousand years, until the Second Vatican Council. Western European Christianity, stemming from Greco-Roman thought patterns, has been the predominant form of Christianity. When the missionaries traveled to the Americas or to Africa, this was the form of Christianity that traveled with them. The Latin mass, for example, was celebrated uniformly throughout the western Catholic world from the time of the Council of Trent until Vatican II.

With Vatican II, however, we enter the third epoch, present and uncharted, which Rahner calls the world church. This means that the Catholic Church, while still remaining Roman, is becoming more diverse in the expression and celebration of its one faith, one baptism, one Lord. Vatican II was the first truly international gathering of bishops. The bishops saw themselves as coming from quite different cultures and heritages, all of which had to be appreciated and listened to. They decided to allow the vernacular language and indeed to advocate its use in the liturgy in place of the Latin tongue. This alone, we see in retrospect, had far deeper consequences than could be imagined at the time. It encouraged Asian and African Catholics to pray to God and to celebrate the sacraments in their own languages; it also prompted them to accelerate the translation of scripture and the church's prayer into the language of their society and culture. Liturgical adaptation to local customs and cultures was called for. The church was to be a "church in the modern world" with its rich diversity of cultures.

Rahner speaks of a break or "caesura" between these epochs. Something new is emerging, something exciting and at times dangerous. The strong negative reaction of Archbishop Lefebrve seems to be proving that Rahner is correct. Much was at stake at Vatican II, and the fostering of the vernacular at Mass rather than the universal retention of Latin is one example of a change.

Irony and Tragedy of Inculturation

Even as we proceed to try to understand inculturation, we are struck by the strange feeling that it really should not be necessary to talk about or to study inculturation. Ideally it is something that is ongoing and taken for granted in the proclamation and sharing of the good news. The fact is that lack of adequate inculturation in previous missionary efforts has often resulted in the need to focus on inculturation. In Nigeria today, for example, one is not usually sharing the gospel for the first time with those who have never heard of Jesus Christ. Rather, one encounters a western European form or model of Christianity that is widespread and growing, but a form that is not indigenous to Nigeria. In other words, one has to in some ways de-westernize Christianity, strip it down to the essentials, in order to creatively inculturate gospel values into Nigeria. And this, I suggest, may be much more difficult than inculturation into a society or village that has never heard of Jesus Christ.

The reason for this ironic situation is that, when Christianity went from Europe to the Americas and to Africa, it often traveled with the colonizers. Armed with the myth of the superiority of western European culture, they simply transplanted western Christianity to American and African soil, showing little respect, and often disdain, for traditional local cultures. Bishop Peter Sarpong of Kumasi, Ghana expressed this sentiment in an address to a eucharistic congress a few years ago.

Alas, he [the African] searches in vain for his heart's desire in the Catholic Church. The Christian Church in its wake abolishes his cherished institutions through which he was himself. In fact, the drums and African dances were completely

proscribed as unbecoming of a Christian. Puberty
and initiation ceremonies, the mainstay of juvenile
morality, communal festivity, and social solidarity,
were condemned by "Christianity" as repulsive, re-
pugnant, abhorrent, ridiculous, etc.

We are now able to lament that at its inception,
"Christianity" did not realize that the African
ground had long been carefully prepared by God
for the reception of the Christian seed; and that
that seed had in the course of the centuries inevitably put on the cultural garments of different civili-
zations, Jewish, Greek, Roman, etc.[5]

Thus the church today, in view of the imperative of inculturation, must often undo what has been done poorly, must
reevangelize what was badly evangelized when the gospel was
presented in western European categories and thought
patterns.

As a general rule, we are asserting that inculturation
should occur naturally and spontaneously, wherever the gospel is lived and shared. It should not be something added on,
something optional, something for the classroom or laboratory, but rather the ever-present attitude in all Christian life
and mission. In the final analysis, therefore, inculturation
refers to the correct way of living and sharing one's Christian
faith in a particular context or culture.[6]

On the first level, inculturation is the ongoing way of
engaging in Christian life and mission. This engagement
takes place within families, schools, seminaries, and parishes,
whether in the United States or in Africa. The second level,
the critical, reflective study of inculturation in the
classroom, only makes sense if it leads back to and reinforces
the vision that wherever Christians are, they are inevitably
and inescapably involved in the process of inculturation—

that is, the living and sharing of gospel values in a particular context with its own specific problems and possibilities. Unless inculturation continually returns to the basic level of lived experience, it falls into the danger of being simply another academic ivory-tower exercise, unattached, unrooted, and ineffective.

2. Inculturation and Other Words

As indicated in the previous chapter, the focus on inculturation is something new, occurring only in the past
fifteen years. Yet the reality of inculturation goes back to the
life of Jesus and the preaching of the early church as seen in
the missionary activity of Saint Paul. Because the topic is
developing and under discussion, at present we can expect
no full and final answers. In this chapter I will first try to
clarify the meaning of inculturation by contrasting and
comparing it with related words. Then I will amplify its
meaning by pointing to several images that describe the work
of inculturation.

Inadequate Words

The first three words to be discussed are less than adequate in conveying what inculturation involves. Yet they do
constitute a progressive description of the missionary activity
of the church that approaches more closely the full reality of
inculturation.[1]

1. *Imposition:* This term clearly has a negative meaning.
It refers to a method or process by which doctrines, religious
customs, morals, and ways of praying and acting are brought
from outside, from a foreign or alien culture and tradition,
and imposed or forced upon the new culture. It shows no
appreciation, no respect or regard, for the values, customs,
and religious traditions of the group that is the object of
mission.

Its root meaning is to "place over," and this is exactly

what happens. The new religion or gospel is set over or imposed on the old culture and is never given the opportunity to take root. The assumption is that Christianity must be accepted in the form in which it is offered, whether that be Irish, French, or German Catholicism. If Saint Paul had lost his struggle over circumcision for the Gentiles, then we could say that circumcision would have been imposed as a religious obligation on a culture that neither wanted it nor understood its significance.

The problem with imposition is that it sees Christianity as a finished product, or package, that can be neatly exported from one culture to another. All that might be needed is to translate the writing on the package. In this view the church becomes like most colonial powers, believing that it has the truth embodied in a superior culture, and that those it encounters are inferior and without true values or a significant cultural heritage. Imposition has frequently been the preferred mode of missionary activity because it is safe and easy. The exporters of Christianity remain in control, creating a one-way street.

2. *Translation:* A second term used to describe missionary activity is "translation." This is a necessary starting point, for obviously some translation is necessary, some degree of communication between the old and new cultures. The danger is that translation becomes not only the starting point but the only method. That is, the entire catechism, the prayers and liturgy, and the Bible are simply translated into the new languages with no creative adaptation or modification in accord with local customs or thought patterns. Pope Paul VI echoes this method in his letter "Evangelization in the Modern World," where he writes that the individual churches "have the task of assimilating the essence of the gospel message and transposing it, without the slightest be-

trayal of its essential truth, into the language that these particular people understand, then of proclaiming it in this language."[2]

Translation can involve not only words, but also symbols; for example, the colors and symbols of liturgical vestments can be changed to reflect the local culture. But even this is far from adequate, because it remains on the surface level. Walking a one-way street, the pastoral agent does not enter deeply into the local situation. He or she forgets that to translate literally often means betraying the true meaning of the text or symbol. In reality a foreign culture and tradition is still being imposed on the local one. Furthermore, it is usually assumed that Christ is not part of the new culture at all; he comes as one translated into the new situation, rather than as one already there in hidden ways. He is brought with the pastoral agent and translated into the new culture.

3. *Adaptation:* This term refers to a more creative method of pastoral activity, by which we try to adapt the message we share and the liturgy we celebrate to the customs of those we work among. To adapt means to "make fit," and this implies more serious listening to and study of the culture involved.

Adaptation has been a basic principle of much missionary activity throughout the church's history and is highlighted in the Second Vatican Council. Several passages from the documents of Vatican II speak positively of its necessity. The Constitution on the Sacred Liturgy speaks of adaptation as a basic principle in all liturgical reform (nos. 38–39) and then of the need for a more radical adaptation (no. 40). Likewise, the Decree on the Missionary Activity of the Church advocates understanding the philosophy and wisdom of a new culture, customs, social order, and outlook on life: "As a result, avenues will be opened for a more

profound adaptation in the whole area of Christian life . . ."
(no. 22). Pope Paul VI also called for a more radical adaptation, a call echoed by Pope John Paul II:

> An adaptation of the Christian life in the fields of
> pastoral, ritual, didactic and spiritual activities is
> not only possible, it is even favored by the church.
> . . . In this sense you may, and you must, have an
> African Christianity.[3]

Yet adaptation has more recently been criticized as inadequate, in fact as a subtle form of imposition, and accused
of not truly taking the local culture seriously. Instead of
getting inside, critics say, it remains outside or above, and is
only willing to make or allow extrinsic, accidental, superficial
changes in ways of being Christian. Aylward Shorter writes
that adaptation has come to convey "an activity that is peripheral, non-essential, and even superficial. It was realized
that the concept of 'adaptation' contained within itself the
seeds of perpetual Western superiority and domination."[4]
     Adaptation also seems to presume not only that there is
a definite kernel or center of the gospel, but that it can be
clearly known. This center remains the same, untouched,
while peripheral expressions can change or be adapted. We
must examine later this crucial problem of the kernel, or
center, of Christian faith and life.
     One specific occasion where adaptation was called into
question was in 1974 in Rome at the International Synod on
Evangelization. Here the African bishops declared "completely out of date the so-called theology of adaptation."[5]
The new strategy to be adopted was incarnation of the gospel into African culture—a process more difficult, more
creative, and more dangerous.

More Adequate Words

We now turn to the word incarnation, and to others that go beyond the inadequate words we have discussed, moving toward a more adequate understanding of inculturation.

1. *Indigenization:* To be indigenous means to be a native, one who is born into a particular context or culture. This contrasts, therefore, with the outsider, the translator, or the adapter. We think immediately of indigenous priests or clergy, that is, those who grow up with and know the culture from inside, those who live and understand Christianity from that insider's perspective. The indigenization of theology means that the local community, with its own indigenous leadership, has the primary responsibility and task of developing the teaching, the liturgy, and the practice of that local church. Outside help may be needed at the beginning and at key stages, but the major work is done by the local church as it develops its own identity based on its own cultural heritage and situation. Links with the larger church will continue to encourage the local church, and to ensure that it remains in faithful yet creative continuity with the universal church.

Indigenization reminds us that those coming from outside, the expatriates, will always to some extent remain that —outsiders. Although they have resources and expertise to offer, it is finally the task of the indigenous community and its leadership to form the local church.

One possible danger inherent in the term indigenization is that it might result in too static a view of culture. That is, those within the culture surely know it best, from inside, but they may not be sufficiently aware of the ongoing changes in the culture that are effected by modernization, technology, education, et al. This lack of awareness need not be the case. We must all be aware that cultures are changing, and hence that inculturation is an ongoing process.

2. *Contextualization:* A word that does take into account precisely this changing nature of culture is the term contextualization. Literally the word means a "weaving together," thus an interweaving of the gospel with every particular situation. Instead of speaking of a particular culture, whether traditional or modern, it speaks of contexts or situations into which the gospel must be inculturated.

Contextualization achieved prominence in 1957 when the Rockefeller Foundation gave three million dollars to establish a theological education fund to train leaders for churches in the third world. Grants were offered with a view to "contextualizing the gospel." The World Council of Churches (WCC) in 1972 in Geneva made use of the term, as did the WCC Conference in Lausanne in 1974. In 1978 an International Colloquium on Contextual Theology was held in Manila. More recent writings, such as those of Robert Schreiter, show a preference for this term.[6]

The reference to contexts rather than cultures reminds us that every particular context calls for creative theological reflection. Any particular parish or diocese, retreat house or city, will have a different context and hence may call for a different theological and ministerial response than a neighboring parish or diocese. Contextualization thus shows greater awareness of the particularity of contexts; it also shows greater awareness of the historical development and change that is ongoing in all contexts. One must again and again study the situation and contextualize the gospel for that situation as it changes.

A possible danger of this term is that it may overemphasize the present context to the detriment of continuity with the past. Others say that its emphasis on the ever-changing particular context results in a chameleon-like theology that lacks constancy and solidity.

3. *Incarnation:* The most directly theological word to express the meaning of inculturation is incarnation. "The Word became flesh and dwelt among us" (Jn 1:14). From this gospel text the word incarnation takes on its original depth significance. The Son of God, conceived by the power of the Spirit, is born of Mary. Incarnation refers to the entire Christ-event—the coming, birth, growth, daily life and struggle, teaching, healing, resting, celebrating, suffering, dying, and rising of Jesus Christ. Paul speaks of the mystery of incarnation in the letter to the Philippians. He explains that this attitude of self-emptying, the attitude of Jesus Christ, should also be the attitude of the Christian (Phil 2:5–11).

Jesus was born, lived, and died in a particular context or culture. He learned the language and customs, and in and through these he expressed the truth and love of God. He did not consciously indigenize or inculturate, but instinctively took part fully in the culture he was born into, and then critically affirmed and challenged that culture in light of the Spirit. According to Samuel Rayan, "He was just being himself there as the concrete saving presence and self-giving of God to them."[7] This stance becomes the model for Christian mission today. As Pedro Arrupe writes:

> The Incarnation of the Son is the primary motivation and perfect pattern for inculturation. Just like him, and because he did so, the Church will become incarnate as vitally and intimately as it can in every culture, being enriched with its values and offering it the unique redemption of Christ, his message and the resources for a new life.[8]

Recent official Roman Catholic teaching seems to call for this way of understanding inculturation. The following statement is made in the Second Vatican Council's Decree on the Missionary Activity of the Church:

> If the church is to be in a position to offer all men the mystery of salvation and the life brought by God, then it must implant itself among all these groups in the same way that Christ by his incarnation committed himself to the particular social and cultural circumstances of the men among whom he lived (*Ad Gentes*, no. 1).

In the same document (no. 22) the young churches are called to "imitation of the plan of the incarnation." More recently Pope John Paul II, addressing the bishops of Nigeria, spoke of the divine message being incarnated and communicated through the culture of each people. When he returned to Rome after his visit to Africa, he declared that "African culture is a splendid substratum which awaits the incarnation of Christianity."[9]

Incarnation, therefore, presents us not with an option but an obligation. As followers of Jesus Christ, we are to identify ourselves with the culture, people, and history we are part of. We are to live with both feet on the ground, taking seriously God's creation and the human re-creation of that world through culture. For it is only in and through particular cultures and contexts that God's love and truth are revealed and made present.

4. *Inculturation:* We turn now to the word that is at the center of our discussion, namely, inculturation. The exact origins of the term as it functions in the theological community remain unclear. Cardinal Sin of Manila used it at the Synod on Catechesis held in Rome in 1977. It was first

included in an official papal document by John Paul II, in his Apostolic Exhortation on Catechesis of October 1979. Since then it has become commonplace. The final report from the Extraordinary Synod of 1985 contains a section on inculturation. Pope John Paul mentions it frequently, especially in his journeys to Africa.

At its best, the term combines the theological significance of incarnation with the anthropological concepts of enculturation and acculturation to create something new. One of its advantages is that it is still open and malleable. The related and more traditional word *enculturation* is used by anthropologists. This word refers to the process of learning about a new cultural tradition through, for example, the process of socialization into that new culture. It is the process by which an individual becomes inserted into his or her culture. Inculturation is not the same as enculturation, because in the case of inculturation the Christian does not come empty-handed, but has a specific tradition to bring to the new situation.

Acculturation, again as used by anthropologists and social scientists, refers to contact or encounter between two cultures and the changes that result. But here too there is a difference from inculturation, because the church or the Christian tradition is not in our view simply another culture, but has its own special nature and mission. And the process of inculturation, as we will see, calls not only for contact but for insertion.

Yet the process of inculturation has much to learn from the social sciences, and in particular from cultural anthropology, which teaches us the various meanings of culture, the theories that account for cultural divergences, and how to understand or interpret a culture. The very word culture is problematic, with no fixed, agreed-upon definition. In general we may describe it as "a set of symbols, stories, (myths) and norms for conduct that orient a society or group cognitively, affectively, and behaviorally to the world in which it lives."[10]

Now that we have presented a working definition of inculturation, we can indicate some of the positive advantages of this way of describing the Christian mission. First, instead of adhering to more deductive understandings of culture and more philosophical, universal understandings of human nature, inculturation introduces us to the data of the social sciences such as cultural anthropology, sociology, and ethnology. Second, it leads to a fruitful dialogue or interchange between culture and gospel/church, as called for by the Second Vatican Council, most explicitly in the Pastoral Constitution on the Church in the Modern World. Third, it moves beyond imposition, translation, and adaptation toward the reorientation, renewal, and transformation of culture from within in light of the gospel message. Finally, the notion of inculturation underlines the central role of the local church and community in the mission of the church in the modern world.

It must be noted too that inculturation should not be limited to some particular area of Christian life and mission. Rather it involves all aspects of being a Christian. When we hear of inculturation we probably think first of the area of liturgy. This of course, is a key area, and a highly visible one. The language, music, vestments, style, and form of the liturgy should reflect the local culture. But inculturation extends far wider than that. In the words of Archbishop D. S. Lourdusamy:

> Every aspect of the life and activity of the church should be incultured or indigenous: indigenous

life-style, indigenous arts, liturgy, spirituality, indigenous forms of religious life, indigenous organizations and institutions.

The way theology is studied and written about, the way children are taught the rudiments of the faith, the way the parish council is structured, the way the diocese is organized, the architecture of churches, the shape and form of prayers—all of these areas fall under the scope of inculturation. In a later chapter on inculturation in the church of Nigeria, we will touch on some of these areas.

Concrete Images of Inculturation

Jesus taught with imagery taken from his culture, pointing to the birds of the air, the lilies of the field, the sower and the seed, and so on, to explain the mysteries of the kingdom. Concrete imagery can also be used to describe the meaning of inculturation and the mission of the church. In this section we will examine several images that help to reveal the reality and process of inculturation.

Salt: You are the salt of the earth. As Christians bearing the gospel enter a new situation, they must be seen as preserving, not destroying, the positive values of that new culture. Salt is a preservative and also brings out the flavor of food. Likewise the gospel should elicit or bring forth the best that is already present in a culture. Inculturation, accordingly, does not destroy but rather strives to preserve and to build on the values already present in a given culture.

Leaven: The gospel acts as a leaven, enabling growth and expansion as it enters a new situation. Just as yeast enables the dough to rise and become a loaf of bread, so the gospel assists in the transformation of cultures. In quiet, often hidden ways it makes a difference, acting not from without but from within the culture.

Seed: This image, again biblically rooted, becomes more complex and variable. The gospel, the Christian message, is the seed that should eventually germinate, grow, and bear fruit. The resulting tree becomes large enough to provide shade, comfort, and a nesting place for the birds of the field. But a key question must be asked: Is the seed of the gospel brought from outside the culture (from Rome or Ireland to Africa), or is it already present in hidden ways in the culture? There is quite a difference between these two perspectives. If the seed comes from outside, then it may never truly fit into the new, always remaining foreign and in some ways imposed. But if, as Vatican II says, the seeds of the word are already present throughout the world, then the perspective shifts.[12] The work of the pastoral agent is not to import seed, but rather to search for and uncover the seed already there, to encourage and to name it and to help it grow and blossom in its own soil. The hidden Christ has already touched the culture; the pastoral agent makes this known, and in the process fosters growth and the bearing of fruit.

Planting: A related image for the mission of the church is that of planting. Used heavily before Vatican II, it is also found in the letters of Paul. "I planted, Apollos watered, but God gave the growth" (1 Cor 3:6). As with the image of the seed, though, one must ask if the plant comes from outside or from within the culture. Is it transplanted from Europe, or is it a native plant that is nurtured? The more open and radical view of inculturation would insist that the plant is indigenous to the new culture. One African bishop stated that the priority in mission is not to transplant the western tree in Africa or Asian soil, but to plant and nourish our own tree and do what is required for its vitality and health.[13]

Catalyst: A contemporary image is that of the catalyst. A

catalyst is something added to a situation that produces a reaction but remains itself unchanged. The truth of this image would be that the pastoral agent assists in the process of something new occurring, like a chemical agent or catalyst, as one who helps but does not dominate. The coming and presence of the pastoral agent provide the opportunity for the people already there to discover for themselves the richness of the gospel. The people are ultimately responsible for their life and faith, and like a catalyst the pastoral agent accompanies them in this process of discovery.

Pilgrim: A pilgrim is someone on a journey, searching. The mystery of God, the mystery of the gospel, is never fully fathomed, and we journey together as a pilgrim people. As a fellow pilgrim the pastoral agent does not cling to the past, but optimistically hopes and searches for a new future. The pastoral agent enters the new culture to facilitate, to walk with others in their common search. This image, we may note, replaces the unhealthy image of the conquistador. The conquistador comes with all the answers, with no desire to listen but instead with the colonialist mentality that the culture one brings is superior, and the traditional culture inferior. This attitude, we must admit, was prominent in the early history of the church in Latin America. But it has been or should be replaced, as liberation theology demands, by a theology of accompaniment, of walking together on pilgrimage.

From pearl merchant to hunter for treasure: An older view of missionary activity saw it as bringing the new pearl of great price to a foreign people untouched by the truth and grace of God. The missionary had the answers and shared or imposed them on the ignorant. A newer image would be that of the hunter for treasure. This missionary begins with a much more positive view of the culture he or she enters. He or she helps the people in a search or hunt that is mainly their own. The people must do the digging into their own culture to find the truths already present. As a fellow searcher, the missionary must be open to the new, engaging in a long, arduous search. When the treasure is found, the missionary can return home to his or her own culture, to share that new treasure as a reverse missionary.[14]

Be, beget, be gone: A final series of images portrays the work of the pastoral agent. First, the agent must *be* present to, inserted among and bearing witness to the people. This is a slow process of listening before speaking, learning before teaching. Second, the agent must *beget* small groups that share what they see, the riches they uncover in their own culture, and the richness of the gospel as communicated by the pastoral agent. This is the beginning of the local church. The pastoral agent helps Christ to be named and born again into that culture through the small group. Third, the agent should *be gone.* With a small but solid beginning, the leadership is handed over to the local people, the small group. Instead of hanging on and possibly interfering, the agent lets the local church develop on its own terms, at its own pace. Rather than dependence, its independence and yet interdependence with other local churches and with the universal church is encouraged. The agent of inculturation moves to another situation. Be, beget, be gone. Often the third step is the most difficult.

This chapter has served to introduce more fully the concept of inculturation through a series of contrasts, comparisons, and images. We have traced a transition from less adequate terms such as imposition and translation to the deeper and more radical forms of inculturation or incarnation. In the next chapter we will deepen this historical perspective on inculturation by reviewing examples of both positive and negative moments in history when issues of inculturation of the gospel were at stake.

3. Key Moments in History

From these descriptions of the meaning of inculturation through related words and images, we move to a brief survey of some key moments in Christian history that intersect with the theme of inculturation. Our survey will be highly selective and brief; a fuller history would be a project in itself.[1]

Incarnation

As we have seen, inculturation must continually return to the incarnation of Jesus Christ for its paradigm. The Word of God became flesh; he was like us in all things but sin (see Heb 4:15). Jesus was a Jew, immersed in his culture, observing the law and customs of his times, yet critical of some of the Jewish leaders. He spoke out strongly against an overly narrow and legalistic interpretation of the law. The sabbath is for the human person, not the person for the sabbath. His heart went out in a special way toward the poor, the needy, and the sick—so much so that some writers define his incarnation as partisan, maintaining that Jesus identified his mission and his person with the marginated and the weak. Through his words and actions, Jesus proclaimed that the rule of God is at hand. The path to life is life in accord with the values of the kingdom. Because of the power of his teaching and preaching, opposition arose from both religious (Jewish) and state (Roman) leaders. In solidarity with the persecuted, Jesus himself, the righteous one, was tortured and put to death; yet he rose again.

His work did not stop with death, but rather as risen Lord, through the power of the Spirit, he inaugurated the mission of the church. The apostles and disciples he had formed went out, as the story of Pentecost attests, to share the good news in obedience to the mission mandate of Jesus (see Mt 28). Whereas Jesus addressed himself to non-Jews in only a few instances, his followers were to extend his mission, beginning in Jerusalem, to the ends of the earth (see Acts 1:8). Through them the gospel would be preached to persons and places where Jesus himself did not go.

The Council of Jerusalem

With the conversion and subsequent mission of Saint Paul to the Gentiles, a breakthrough occurred. In the threefold division of church history, as described by Rahner, at this time the church entered a new epoch or era, which has important implications for the meaning of inculturation. One focal point, or moment of truth, for the young Christian community came with the Council of Jerusalem. Here the decision was made to allow Gentiles, non-Jews, to become Christians through baptism without imposing on them the Jewish law of circumcision. To that event we now turn.[2]

The relevant events are described in several places in the New Testament, but they do not entirely cohere in all details. Some would argue that two distinct councils were held. The exact date of the council or councils is disputed. But for our purposes the following overview is adequate. Paul was converted around the year 36. His encounter with the risen Lord gave him the special mission to the Gentiles. After three years of preparation in Damascus, he made a visit to Jerusalem and ministered for a few years around Tarsus and Antioch. After his second visit to Jerusalem in 46 with a donation of money to the Jerusalem church, he undertook his first missionary journey (46-49). Paul's mission brought great success, a large number of Gentile conversions. It also led to the problem of the relationship between the Gentile Christians and the Jewish Christians. In dispute were precisely which aspects of the Jewish tradition must be adhered to before one could be baptized as a Christian. Did the Gentiles first have to become Jews before they would be allowed to become Christians? More specifically, Jewish dietary laws were in question, and, above all, the law of circumcision.

To solve the dispute, a council assembled in Jerusalem in the year 49. The Judaizers held that circumcision, as enjoined in the Old Testament, was necessary for salvation. Paul and his followers maintained that faith in Jesus Christ, and baptism in his name, was the way to salvation (see Acts 15). Peter's position, which agreed with Paul's, prevailed, and it was decided not to lay extra burdens on Gentile converts. Because of this liberating decision, the mission of Paul continued with great success, and the church expanded far beyond the borders of Palestine. One did not first have to become Jewish in order to become Christian. The church would spread to Rome, the center of the Roman empire, and not remain a small Jewish sect, a sect that would have had a dark future in light of the subsequent destruction of Jerusalem in the year 70.

It is simply impossible to conceive of the growth and expansion of Christianity if this liberating decision had not been reached at the Council of Jerusalem. For it affirmed that the center of the gospel is Jesus Christ and faith in him. And it stands as a clear reminder to the church today that not all the customs and traditions of the western, European church must be observed by Christians from non-European cultures. The decision of the Council of Jerusalem enabled the church to proceed (in Rahner's categories) from the first epoch of Jewish Christianity to the second epoch of Gentile Christianity. Significantly, in the present it allows and challenges the church to advance from the second to the third epoch, namely that of the world church.

Through the labors of Paul and other early missionaries, the church did spread throughout the Roman empire. It survived periods of calm and periods of intense persecution. Under Constantine, in the year 313, Christianity was officially tolerated. In 380 under Emperor Theodosius, Christianity was not only tolerated but legally favored. It became an advantage, as a Roman citizen, to be a Christian. These two developments resulted in shifts in the relationship between the church and culture, and thus had great significance for inculturation. In them we see the church moving from a position of persecution by the state to one of acceptance and even preference by the state and dominant culture. On the one hand, this state sponsorship enabled the tremendous growth of the church. On the other hand, it led to possible identification of the church with the state, manipulation of the church by the state, and the loss of a critical Christian contribution to the state or dominant culture.

It is interesting to note that as the missionary activity of the church intensified at the end of the sixth century, a question similar to that raised at the Council of Jerusalem surfaced during the papacy of Gregory the Great. Pope Gregory had been instrumental in initiating the mission to England, and in 596 he dispatched Augustine and a group of monks to Canterbury. A few years later he wrote a famous letter on the methods of the missionary. Instead of condemnation of the customs of the Angles and Saxons, there was to be critical interaction and accommodation. The pope's letter was written to Mellitus, an abbot in France, who was about to join Saint Augustine of Canterbury as a fellow missionary:

> Tell Augustine that he should by no means destroy the temples of the gods but rather the idols within those temples. Let him, after he has purified them with holy water, place altars and relics of the saints in them. For if those temples are well built, they should be converted from the worship of demons to the service of the true God. Thus, seeing that their places of worship are not destroyed, the people will banish error from their hearts and come to places familiar and dear to them in acknowledgment and worship of the true God.[3]

He continues that instead of totally eliminating sacrifice from the culture, the Christians should transform local festivals into religious feasts and celebrations of thanksgiving. As the pope admits, it is impossible to effect radical changes all at once and one must proceed slowly and by stages. This more gentle and accommodating posture, we must note, was not often followed in the history of the church's mission.

Christianity and Philosophy

Saint Paul spoke critically of the wisdom of the Greek philosophers, contrasting it with the wisdom of Jesus Christ, which centered on the folly of the cross. Later Christians, among them Justin Martyr, viewed some of the pagan philosophers as anticipating the gospel, because they perceived the seeds of divine truth and revelation in their thoughts and writings. Saint Augustine learned much from Greek philosophers such as Plotinus, and used them in his own writings.

Above all, Thomas Aquinas is a model for the Christian appropriation of non-Christian philosophers. In the thirteenth century there was a new influx of Aristotelian texts into Europe. Aristotle was pagan and pre-Christian, yet his thought captivated many, especially at the University of Paris where Thomas studied and taught. Instead of dismissing out of hand the thought of Aristotle, Thomas studied it carefully and commented on it extensively, criticizing it and using it creatively in his presentation of the Christian faith. He distinguished between truth and error, the values that were compatible with Christianity and those that were not. By this critical appropriation of Aristotle's thought (as well as that of other Greek philosophers) Thomas was able to forge a new synthesis of Christianity—one that has lasted through the centuries. In the language of inculturation, Thomas listened openly to the new ideas, new methods, and new culture that came with Aristotle. He evaluated them and accepted the true and the good, seeing that the same God who spoke through Jesus Christ could also speak through the writings of this pagan philosopher.

Two additional remarks should be added to this brief discussion of Thomas. First is the fact that, soon after his death, several of his ideas were condemned by the archbishop of Paris. Creative theological reflection—and inculturation calls for this—is continually in danger of being misunderstood or wrongly judged; time would vindicate Thomas Aquinas. A second fact worth noting is that Archbishop Helder Cámara of Recife, Brazil called for the retrieval of the boldness of Thomas Aquinas in a speech delivered at the University of Chicago in 1974.[4] Addressing a symposium in honor of Thomas Aquinas, he challenged his audience to do in our day what Thomas did in his, namely, to engage in dialogue with, to listen to, to learn from, and to criticize the leading ideas of the times. Cámara was referring especially to Marxist thought, saying that it cannot simply be dismissed (it is too powerful for that), nor must it be uncritically accepted. This as we will see is being done, though not without opposition, by a number of theologians throughout Latin America today.

Missionary Expansion from the Fifteenth to the Seventeenth Century

With the explorers from Europe traveling to India and the Americas went the Christian missionaries. Both explorers and missionaries often had the same negative attitude toward those they encountered. Their conviction of the superiority of European culture and European religion was deeply ingrained. One particularly abominable expression of this conviction occurs in the papal bull of Nicholas V in 1452 to the king of Portugal:

> In the name of our apostolic authority, we grant to you the full and entire faculty of invading, conquering, expelling and reigning over all the kingdoms, the duchies . . . of the Saracens, of pagans and of all infidels, wherever they may be found; of reducing their inhabitants to perpetual slavery, of appropriating to yourself those kingdoms and all their possessions, for your own use and that of your successors.[5]

This view contrasts sharply with the more positive and accommodating view expressed at the beginning of the seventh century by Pope Gregory the Great. Because of the assumption of superiority manifested in the bull of Pope Nicholas V, much of the traditional culture in areas of North and South America was destroyed as the colonial conquest expanded. This would be an example of imposition rather than inculturation or even accommodation.

The Council of Trent

As a late response to the reformation, the Council of Trent assembled in 1540. The official Catholic reaction at Trent to the new ways of thinking, to the split within Christendom, and to the new world that was opened up by the sailing ships was one of consolidation and standardization. The catechism was standardized, the rites of the liturgy, kept in Latin, were made uniform, and, very importantly, the training of future priests was to be done in seminaries, which would have their own life and existence somewhat separated from the universities and cultural centers. Positively, Trent strengthened the Catholic world, but, negatively, it rigidified Catholic teaching, stressing the center, Europe and Rome, at the expense of the expanding world with its differences of traditions and cultures.

Matteo Ricci and Roberto de Nobili

Two noteworthy exceptions to the common missionary practice of disregarding the local culture are found in the missionary work of two Jesuits. Matteo Ricci (1552–1610) was a missionary to China. He realized that if Christianity were to enter deeply into the life of China, it had to find points of contact with Confucianism. He adopted the attitude that Justin Martyr had taken toward Greek thought in the second century, namely that elements of truth in the culture with which one is in dialogue should be preserved. Through his knowledge of mathematics and science, he gained entry into the intellectual circles of China, almost reaching the emperor himself. He studied the Chinese philosophers and tried to use their language and images to understand and teach Christian doctrine.

Like Paul, he desired to be all things to all men and women. Thus he wrote to his superior in Rome:

> To gain greater status we do not walk along the streets on foot, but have ourselves carried in sedan chairs, on men's shoulders, as men of rank are accustomed to do. For we have great need of this type of prestige in this region, and without it would make no progress among these gentiles; for the name of foreigners and priests is considered so vile in China that we need this and other similar devices to show them that we are not priests as vile as their own.[6]

Opposition to this approach to missionary activity grew, and it had to be abandoned when Rome rejected the development of native rites and opposed other cultural adaptations in the Chinese Rites controversy.

Roberto de Nobili, another Italian Jesuit missionary, went to India in 1605. He decided that it would help his mission if he imitated the sannyasi, the holy men of India, by adopting their dress, speech, diet, and way of life. He studied the Hindu scriptures and made many converts. Yet opposition to his approach also grew, and investigations were ordered. In spite of opposition from within India, Rome pronounced in de Nobili's favor in the so-called Malabar Rites controversy, after thirteen bitter years. He died in 1656, and only three years later in 1659 the following statement was made by the Congregation for the Propagation of the Faith to the vicars apostolic of China:

> Do not waste your zeal or your powers of persuasion in getting these people to change their rites, customs, or ways of life, unless these be very ob-

viously opposed to faith and morals. For what could be more ridiculous than to import France, Spain, Italy or any other part of Europe into China? What you carry with you is not a national culture but a message which does not reject or offend the sound traditions of any country, but rather wants to safeguard and foster them.[7]

With sound wisdom, the directive continues that it is in the nature of human persons to want the customs of their country to be esteemed, loved, and respected above anything else in the world. It notes that trying to change these customs will result in alienation and hatred. Again with a deep sensibility, it advises against making comparisons between the customs of Asians and those of Europeans, warning that one should be prudent enough not to pass judgment on Asian customs, and certainly not to condemn them rashly or exaggeratedly.

This profound and deeply pastoral statement echoes that of Gregory the Great, and shows a remarkable openness to what we now call inculturation. It is a milestone in the history of missiology. Yet how well it was received and implemented remains another question.

Vatican I

With the First Vatican Council (1869–1870), we see not interaction between church and culture, but rather withdrawal and retrenchment on the part of the church. Fear of modern ideas, new liberal attitudes, and the influence of the enlightenment led the Catholic Church toward centralization and further standardization. The papacy received new power and emphasis at the expense of the local churches under their bishops. Even though the council reaffirmed the

Catholic emphasis upon faith *and* reason, it was very wary of contemporary intellectual movements and issued condemnations rather than calls for dialogue. We might note that the First Vatican Council was composed of bishops who were almost all Europeans, or at least born in Europe. Although the church was spread far over the world, as a world church it was not adequately represented at Vatican I. This is in sharp contrast to the composition of the Second Vatican Council, which we will examine below.

The promulgation of the Code of Canon Law in 1917 had a similar thrust. Although it served to unify the various codes in existence, a necessary task, it also created uniformity and minimized pluralism and diversity in canon law, showing little regard for differences of cultures and traditions.

The century between the two Vatican Councils was a period of intense missionary activity, which witnessed the founding of a number of missionary orders, several of them with a particular focus on Africa. Instructions from Rome and papal encyclicals on the missions were also issued. One strong emphasis of this period was on the establishment of the local clergy, soon to be followed by the local bishop or hierarchy. In 1919 Pope Benedict XV saw this as the greatest hope of the new churches. He recognized that the local priests have access to places where foreign priests are not tolerated and that they understand the mentality and aspirations of their own people. He also prescribed that the local clergy be trained not simply to act as assistants to foreign priests, but to take up God's work as equals.[8]

Pius XI encouraged the establishment of indigenous religious communities of both men and women. He foresaw that these communities would be more in keeping with the local character and temperament, and thus better suited to the particular needs of a given area. In addition, he exhorted the superiors of contemplative orders to establish monasteries in missionary regions.[9]

Pius XII continued in the same direction. The aim of missionary activity, he proclaimed, is supernatural union in an all-embracing love, and not a uniformity that can only be external and superficial and therefore weak. Again, he called for the preservation and development of local usages and customs that are not clearly erroneous. In addition to promoting the development of the local clergy, Pius XII enlisted the assistance of the laity through Catholic Action in the mission of the church.[10] The various writings of these popes prepared the way for the new breakthrough that was to occur at the Second Vatican Council. Gradually the work of the missions had been shifting to the local church. The number of African, Asian, and Latin American priests and bishops was growing. The stage was being set for Pope John XXIII to open the windows and welcome the fresh air of the Spirit more deeply into the church. To achieve this goal he convoked the Second Vatican Council.

Vatican II

According to the interpretation of Karl Rahner, with Vatican II we begin a new, third epoch or era in Christian history, the coming of the world church. During the pontificate of Pope John XXIII major shifts occurred both in the church itself and in the relation of the church to the modern world. The setting for the discussion of these changes was St. Peter's, in Rome, where the more than two thousand council fathers assembled. Many of these bishops came from Africa, Asia, and Latin America. The universality and catholicity of the Roman church became visible with the presence and representation of so many different cultures and traditions.

The council itself was an exercise in inculturation as the church tried to open its windows to the modern world, with its joys and sorrows, hopes and anxieties. Many of the official documents of the council should be studied with respect to their implications for inculturation, but we will briefly mention only a few.[11]

The Constitution on the Sacred Liturgy called for the revision of the liturgy in accord with particular situations and cultures. The vernacular could be used in place of the universal Latin language. As we see now, this was not a small change but a radical shift from the center to the periphery, which released a new spirit of creativity in the local church. Symbols, rites, and prayers were to be revised to harmonize more with local situations. Instead of total uniformity among all churches, the principle of adaptation was approved and encouraged (nos. 37–40).

The Pastoral Constitution on the Church in the Modern World, though it did not use the word inculturation, did speak extensively of culture—of the gap between religion and culture and the need to bridge that gap. It advocated a listening, dialogical attitude with culture, both traditional and modern:

> Sent to all peoples of every time and place, the church is not bound exclusively to any race or nation, nor to any particular way of life or customary pattern of living, ancient or recent. Faithful to its own tradition and at the same time conscious of its universal mission, it can enter into communion with various cultural modes, to its own enrichment and theirs too (no. 58).

As the church works for the true development of cultures (nos. 53–62) it not only contributes but also learns and receives from them (no. 44).

The Decree on the Missionary Activity of the Church takes the incarnation of Jesus Christ as the paradigm of missionary activity, but it also affirms that the seeds of the Word are already present in particular cultures. It calls for a more profound adaptation, including the evaluation of local cultures and customs and the retention of what is good and holy (nos. 21–22). This document is indispensable for the study of inculturation, since it brings together the best of recent papal teaching on the meaning and methods of missionary activity.

The Decree on the Apostolate of the Laity, as well as several other documents, emphasizes that it is not through the clergy but through the laity that the church will be present in modern society and culture, through the laity who are committed, trained, involved, and engaged in business, educational institutions, politics, and local communities. This role of the laity, as we will see, has significant implications for the process of inculturation in developing nations, and perhaps even more in the developed or overdeveloped nations.

Pope Paul VI and Pope John Paul II

The thrust and direction of Vatican II have been continued by subsequent popes. On his worldwide travels as pope, Paul VI personally demonstrated the concern and interest of the church in all peoples. The first pope to visit Africa, in 1969 he challenged the Africans: "By now, you Africans are missionaries to yourselves."[12] In the same document he spoke strongly of the need for adaptation. We quote extensively from this document, since it is so powerful and so significant for the process of inculturation. While the faith is one,

> the expression, that is, the language and mode of manifesting this one faith, may be manifold; hence it may be original, suited to the tongue, the style, the character, the genius, and the culture, of the one who professes this one faith. From this point of view, a certain pluralism is not only legitimate, but desirable. An adaptation of the Christian life in the fields of pastoral, ritual, didactic and spiritual activities is not only possible, it is even favored by the church. The liturgical renewal is a living example of this. And in this sense you may, and you must, have an African Christianity.[13]

Paul VI continued in this mode with his apostolic exhortation, "The Evangelization of Peoples" issued on December 8, 1975, after the International Synod of Bishops which had discussed the topic of evangelization in 1974. He warned of the dangerous split between gospel and culture (no. 20) and called positively for the evangelization of cultures: "What matters is to evangelize man's culture and cultures (not in a purely decorative way, as it were by applying a thin veneer, but in a vital way, in depth and right to their very roots)" (no. 20). The very process of evangelization is a creative process of insertion, incarnation, and inculturation, even though this document does not use the word inculturation. The pope realizes that the success or failure of evangelization is at stake. Thus he explains that "evangelization loses much of its force and effectiveness if it does not take into consideration the actual people to whom it is addressed, if it does not use their language, their signs and symbols, if it does not answer the questions they ask, and if it does not have an impact on their concrete life" (no. 63).

Finally, we turn to Pope John Paul II. The very fact that he is from Poland and not from Italy, as popes had been since the sixteenth century, is significant. It points to the catholicity and universality of the church, even if the church's headquarters are in Rome and the pope is officially the bishop of Rome.

Pope John Paul II uses the word inculturation in many different speeches as he travels throughout the world. In 1980 in Nairobi, Kenya he said,

> Inculturation, which you rightly promote, will truly be a reflection of the incarnation of the word, when a culture, transformed and regenerated by the gospel, brings forth from its own living tradition original expressions of Christian life, celebration, and thought.[14]

He continues most significantly and beautifully that

> there is no question of adulterating the word of God or of emptying the cross of its power (cf. 1 Cor 1:17) but rather of bringing Christ into the very center of African life and of lifting up all African life to Christ. Thus not only is Christianity relevant to Africa, but Christ, in the members of his body, is himself African.

In May 1982 the pope established a Pontifical Council for Culture with an international membership consisting of laymen, laywomen, religious, priests, and bishops. Among the council's functions would be to witness to the holy see's deep interest in the progress of culture and to assist in the dialogue between cultures and the gospel. It advises the pope on questions of culture, and hence on inculturation. In addition to its various projects around the world, this council meets annually in Rome where the pope addresses it.

More recently, the Extraordinary Synod of Bishops meeting in December 1985 reflected on the meaning, significance, and implementation of the Second Vatican Council. In its final report, its message to the people of God, the synod spoke of inculturation as follows: "Inculturation is different from a simple external adaptation, because it means the intimate transformation of authentic cultural values through their integration into Christianity and the establishment of Christianity in the various human cultures."[15]

I have attempted much, most likely too much, in this chapter. Yet my goal was to provide some insight into the changing, developing nature of the church's mission and the challenge of inculturation. The church cannot hide or suppress the mistakes or the narrow views of the past. But it can and must learn from them, and above all from the overall positive side of its history and the successes of its rich tradition.

4. Theological Bases

As indicated earlier, there are cultural and historical reasons for the new focus on inculturation. We are more aware of different traditions and cultures, and we see this diversity as an enriching gift that Catholic theology must build on if it is to be truly catholic and universal. We appreciate the desire to explore one's particular heritage or roots. The melting pot of America, for example, should not exist at the expense of the rich religious and secular customs of the ethnic groups and national heritages that come together to make this nation. Nor should the rush to modernization in third world nations proceed at the cost of the destruction of their traditional values.

This new awareness of culture should go hand in hand with theological awareness. Theology can be described as critical reflection on one's faith, or, in a traditional formulation, as faith seeking understanding. As one's faith is influenced by one's culture, so too is one's theology influenced. But the relationship is mutual, and thus as faith seeks to influence and transform a culture, so too does theology. Theological understandings, therefore, both have an impact on the culture and are affected by the culture. It is this interweaving of theology and culture that we will examine by looking briefly at four key areas of theology and seeing how they can be understood in light of inculturation. The four areas are revelation, grace, christology, and ecclesiology. In each area we will assess changes that have occurred, changes that are significant for our understanding of inculturation.

Revelation

Normally the Christian thinks of revelation primarily as the revelation in scripture, which reached its high point in Jesus Christ. Possibly one thinks of ongoing revelation through the spirit of Jesus in and to the church. While this is the center, it remains a narrow perspective and one that must be expanded in the light of tradition and contemporary understanding. We see now more clearly that God is close to all men and women, and has been throughout human history. In diverse hidden ways God offers light and truth to all men and women. Thus as we have seen, Vatican II speaks of the *semina verbi,* the seeds of the word that are present in all cultures, not only in the Christian tradition.[1] The result of this new understanding is that the agent of inculturation does not enter into godless contexts, but rather steps onto holy ground, insofar as God is already in contact with a given context even if in imperfect and hidden ways. We cannot simply say that we, with the gospel, have the truth of revelation and the non-Christian does not.

Second, we are aware of the mediated, historical nature of God's revelation. Revelation does not enter as universal magic, but rather occurs in particular histories to concrete persons and communities in particular contexts and cultures. Only after its historical entrance is understood and appreciated can we begin to speak of the general or universal implications of revelation. Revelation, God's self-communication and establishment of covenant relationships, takes place in and through cultures. Thus to understand the God who reveals and the self-communication offered, we must pay attention to the historical context or culture. Cultures, both traditional and modern, remain the locus for God's past, present, and future revelation.

Grace

Related to, and inseparable from, the theology of revelation is the theology of grace. Grace, the human person's sharing in the inner life of God, like revelation is offered to all men and women, and any exclusivist understanding of grace would deny the understanding of inculturation as a two-way street, a listening as well as a sharing or teaching. The older, exclusivist understanding of grace accounted for the lack of respect for local cultures and traditional religion, and for the colonialist attitude of much traditional missionary endeavor. If, on the other hand, grace is offered to and is in some ways present in cultures and contexts beyond the explicit Christian pale, then the agent of inculturation must attend to and search for that presence, learn from it and build on it rather than reject or ignore it. Grace and the Holy Spirit are inseparable and universally offered. As the Preface for Christian Unity says so well: "Through Christ you have given the Holy Spirit to all peoples." Karl Rahner can thus say that grace is embedded in reality, so much so that his view of the world has been aptly described as a "world of grace."[2] With the insight of liberation theology, we see too that grace is transformational or liberating. Inculturation of gospel values, that is, graced values, into a context may well call for transformation of particular sinful aspects of a culture or context.

Christology

"God so loved the world that he gave his only Son" (Jn 3:16). Jesus Christ is the sign and reality of God's love not only for Christians, but for all men and women in all cultures

and contexts. A correct understanding of inculturation presupposes, therefore, some theory of what has been called
"the anonymous Christian." That is to say, the love of God in
Christ Jesus is offered to all, and we see and experience it as
active even if in anonymous or hidden ways. God's love in
Christ is present, at least as an offer, before the missionary
or pastoral agent begins his or her mission.[3]

Inculturation must also be attuned to Matthew 25.
There in the parable of the last judgment, Jesus identifies
himself in a special way with the needy, the hungry, the
imprisoned, and the naked. Christ is found not only in the
scriptures, not only in the Christian community, but in a
particular way in the marginated and the poor. This perspective must be part of our way of reading or analyzing
cultures if we are Christians.

Inculturation makes us aware of the particularity of the
incarnation. Jesus was a Jew, born into a specific culture,
time, and place. As he interacted with his culture, religious
and secular, learning from it and criticizing it, so we must do
the same. We do not imitate Jesus to the last detail (how he
dressed or ate), but rather try to focus on the center of his
life and message, that of the reign of God. We note that the
incarnation of Jesus and the proclamation of the reign of
God were addressed especially to the poor, the weak, the
sinners, the needy. In this sense some speak of a partisan
incarnation.

The pattern of the incarnation is the pattern for inculturation. And we must follow the incarnation, as in the example of Jesus, to its end. In his case it led to a life of service,
and eventually to rejection, suffering, death, and finally resurrection. Incarnation in a sinful world will always involve a
painful dying to sin and self, and a living for God and others.
Likewise, inculturation of gospel values may mean dying to
one's limited cultural views and being open to the new, rich

directions in which God calls. Inculturation entails this putting off of the old and putting on of the new. It calls for deep association with the paschal mystery of Jesus Christ, the only way to new life.

Above all, inculturation presupposes and in turn deepens our appreciation of the full and true humanity of Jesus Christ. He was like us in all things but sin (see Heb 2:17–18; 4:14–16). Christian belief in Jesus Christ has often tended to emphasize his divinity, and implicitly to deny or ignore his full humanity. This monophysitic tendency, seeing him simply as God, emphasizes the eternal, ahistorical nature of Jesus. He moves above and apart from all culture, all historical contingency. The true and full meaning of incarnation is denied. If this is one's position, then the task of inculturation is also undercut, and one's faith life is never really inserted into a context, but hovers somehow between heaven and earth, unrooted in the culture, uncommitted to the challenges of history.

Ecclesiology

One's view of church follows closely from one's christology. The church must be seen as both human and divine, and not only as human but also as a church of sinners. Just as exclusive emphasis on the divinity of Jesus is heretical, so is a view of church that overlooks the human element. The church is not yet perfect; but is searching on pilgrimage. Rather than being triumphalistic, it must be a servant church. This serving attitude must be manifest amid the joys and sorrows of human culture and history, not in some separate, ahistorical realm. The church should be ready to admit that it does not have all the answers, and that it has made mistakes in the past in its missionary efforts.

Traditionally we speak of the four notes or marks of the church, namely one, holy, catholic and apostolic. These receive a somewhat different emphasis when set in the context of inculturation. Instead of being seen as already fully possessed by the church, they are seen as gifts of the Spirit, as challenge, and as task. To be catholic means to be open, adaptable, receptive in all contexts and cultures, and this is still to be achieved; in fact, it is an ongoing and never-ending process. Thus Vatican II:

> Sent to all peoples of every time and place, the church is not bound exclusively and indissolubly to any race or nation, nor to any particular way of life or customary pattern of living, ancient or recent. Faithful to her own tradition and at the same time conscious of her universal mission, she can enter into communion with various cultural modes, to her own enrichment and theirs too.[4]

Inculturation, as we will see, is not best carried out by one person, but is the work of the entire community. In this sense the church is viewed as a community of disciples. A disciple is one who learns, and the church community seeks the truth that is always greater, always ahead of it as it moves into new situations and contexts. The laity, as we saw with reference to Vatican II, play a crucial role in the actual living of gospel values in the marketplace and in various cultural situations. If inculturation is to succeed, it will be through the laity. Thus an inculturating church shifts from hierarchy-centered to lay-centered, without denying the necessary but distinctive role of the hierarchy in the mission of the church.

The process of inculturation arising from the community can best be carried out if the church sees itself and organizes itself along the lines of the Latin American basic Christian community model (BCC). This model sees the church as composed primarily of small groups of committed Christians, lay and clergy, in cooperation and collaboration, inserted in and examining their particular situation in order to see how the gospel challenges and speaks to that situation. The life and work of the BCCs offer the church a paradigm, it seems to me, for the task of inculturation.[5]

Ecclesiology in the light of inculturation reminds us that every church is a mission church and every Christian is on mission. In place of the older understanding that some places are the object of mission, and some Christians are missionaries, we now say that all are called and sent, and that means all persons and all churches. There is no authentic church, no authentic Christian without mission, without that sense of being sent to bring gospel values, the good news, to one's particular context and culture.[6]

Roman Catholic Emphasis

We can move one step further, from church to Roman Catholic Church. Here we speak of a specific affinity between the Roman Catholic tradition and inculturation. In contrast to the reformation churches, Catholicism is less pessimistic concerning the nature of the human person after the fall. Catholicism engages in dialogue with philosophy and upholds the natural law tradition. While it believes in the primacy of scripture, it also admits other sources to the theological process, including reason, the arts, and cultural experience. In place of the more Protestant model (according to H.R. Niebuhr) of Christ in paradox with culture, we might say that Catholicism has traditionally represented the position of Christ above culture. More recently with Vatican

II, it has moved strongly toward a model of Christ as transformer of culture. With its heavily sacramental universe—seven sacraments and a host of sacramentals—Catholicism is by nature and by tradition more open to the richness and variety of symbols and signs that point to and embody the divine. Not by escaping from culture and history, but by critically entering into it and dialoguing with it, will the church be truly catholic and universal. In a word, Catholicism represents the analogical rather than the dialectical imagination, and is thus more open to learning from, listening to, and respecting the varied contexts and cultures shaping human history today.[7]

Reading the Signs of the Times

In discussing the theological bases that underlie any authentic theology of inculturation, we must point finally to two critical areas. The first of these is the "signs of the times," and the second is the question of whether there is a discernible center or kernel of the gospel. Both of these areas are crucial, since inculturation tries to let gospel values intersect with and challenge contemporary values and cultures. Thus in reflecting on contemporary situations, we must look for the signs of God's call or presence that are already inherent in those situations. And in examining gospel values, we must have some clarity on what is or is not essential to the gospel. These two concerns flow directly from what we have said about revelation. Revelation, though it reached a high point in the life, death, and resurrection of Jesus Christ, did not end there. God continues to speak through the Spirit to God's people. Thus to discern this ongoing revelation, one area under scrutiny would be the so-called signs of the times.

To begin to understand what is involved in reading the signs of the times, let us turn to the gospels. There Jesus debates with the Pharisees and Sadducees regarding the signs of the times. He accuses some of these leaders of failing to read the signs of the times, especially the sign of God's coming in the life and ministry of Jesus. They can read the signs in the heavens, they look for spectacular signs and wonders, but they fail to see the more important signs and reality before them, the signs of God's love and judgment in the ministry of Jesus (see, for example, Matthew 12:38–42 and 16:1–4). Jesus says no sign will be given except the sign of Jonah.

Juan Luis Segundo has developed this contrast between the theological method of Jesus and that of the Pharisees.[8] Instead of openly, honestly, personally looking at the life and work of Jesus, and judging it in the light of their hearts, the Pharisees become blinded. Lost in the tradition, they judge the life and work of Jesus in light of the past, denying its validity unless they see special signs from heaven. Jesus calls them hypocrites, and strongly challenges them, asking, "Why do you not judge for yourselves what is right?" (Lk 12:57).

Jesus opposes any traditionalism or fundamentalism that looks so much to the past, or to a sacred book, that it overlooks the present revelation and activity of God in the world. It is this openness to the present that Pope John XXIII retrieved during his brief papacy. In his encyclical *Pacem in Terris* he called upon Christians, and indeed all men and women of good will, to read the signs of the times. Among these signs he included the gains in the rights of the working class, the growing participation of women in public life, and the struggle for independence on the part of colonial nations. Through his leadership, the task of interpreting the signs of the times became a task of the Second Vatican

Council and is inscribed in its documents as a task for the church. The list of texts in which this task is described is long. A few key texts are the Constitution on the Church in the Modern World (nos. 4, 11, 36, 44), the Decree on the Apostolate of the Laity (no. 14), and the Decree on Religious Freedom (no. 15). The following are among the signs that must be attended to: the sense of solidarity among all peoples, the desire to promote and restore the sacred liturgy, and the desire for ecumenical unity.

A key ingredient of any theology and of any theological method, therefore, must be attentiveness to reading and interpreting the signs of the times. This is especially true for the theology of inculturation, which examines the virtues and vices, the sinful and graceful aspects of a culture or situation. Precisely because the theology of inculturation is closely modeled on the theology of incarnation, one must examine the signs of the times. The theology of incarnation says that God is found in and through the human and human history. God is incarnate especially in Jesus Christ, but God continues this saving presence in and through the Spirit. The Spirit works in the world, and it is to the world with its joy and hope, its grief and anxiety, that we must turn to do theology. Not by escaping to some other world, not by seeking signs from outside, from heaven, or from the past, but only by faithful immersion and insertion in our contemporary world can we discern the call, the challenge of God to which we must respond. Liberation theology reminds us that this call can be heard clearly today in the cry of the poor, that privileged locus, those marginalized people with whom God identifies, as in the parable of the last judgment in Matthew 25.

"The church has always had the duty of scrutinizing the signs of the times and of interpreting them in the light of the gospel" (Constitution on the Church in the Modern World, no. 4). This activity should happen spontaneously in a theology of inculturation, and should be part of the method of all theology and ministry. It must be carried on by individuals as well as by groups in the church. As a matter of fact, since Vatican II numerous centers have been established to carry on this task. Think tanks, social centers, and institutes at universities gather scholars, social scientists, and theologians who reflect on the culture and context and try to discern the signs of the times, the key movements that affect human lives. They examine the possibilities and the dangers that are present or beginning to surface. Their discernment has become especially important in light of the rapid change, the evolutionary or even revolutionary nature of society today. Nuclear weapons could wipe out life on the whole planet. Communications can enrich or warp the collective consciousness of humanity. Biology and biological engineering have offered startling new control over the quality of human life. Multinational corporations wield power over the lives of millions of people. Women in first world nations and in third world nations are seeking their rightful place in society and in the church, a place that they themselves will have a voice in determining. Traditional values of African cultures are in danger of being lost as these cultures rush headlong toward modernization in an effort to catch up with first world nations. All of these factors call for theological reflection.

To summarize the new perspective of the theology of the signs of the times, we can refer to the words of a Philippine theologian:

> The theology of the signs of the times has as its point of departure, not the scriptural text and not the data of tradition but what is going on in the world. The purpose of reflecting on what is going on in the world is to find out what is *going forward*

in the world. For the believer, what is going forward in the world is developing God's plan, is pushing forward his design for the world. Therefore, this reflection, this theology has several bases. We have spoken of the *empirical basis*—theology has to begin with data, the facts.

This theology takes for granted that its subject matter must begin with man and the history of man. This is where it starts its reflections, and it leads from this reflection to find out what God's mind is on man and his history.[9]

These words remind us that we as church and as Christians are to be a prophetic people. By baptism each Christian shares in the priestly, kingly-servant, and prophetic roles of Jesus Christ. Thus we can speak not only of the priesthood of all believers, but also of the prophethood of all believers. The prophet is one who hears God's call today and then gives witness to that word. Jesus Christ was prophetic; through baptism the church and individual Christians share in his prophetic office (see the Constitution on the Church, nos. 12 and 35). This can be risky and unsettling, but it is in the nature of the pilgrim church, which strives to inculturate gospel values into its own community and into the world.

The Center of Christianity

In order to be able to discern how and where God is speaking today through the signs of the times, it is important to know how and where God spoke in ages past. For Christians, God spoke especially in scripture and in Christian tradition. Yet this itself is problematic. The Bible is complex, composed of many books written over hundreds of years.

The New Testament consists of twenty-eight books, including four gospels, four accounts of the life, death, and resurrection of Jesus Christ. As the church has evolved we have many different forms of the creed, seven sacraments, numerous sacramentals, and 1,752 canons in the new Code of Canon Law. In other words, for two thousand years we have been living, developing, and reflecting on Christian faith.

The question arises; What is at the center, who is so important that all Christians must hold and believe it? Is there a core or kernel or center that must be believed if one is to be considered Christian? To put this in terms of mission and inculturation, what gospel values, what part of the gospel, what aspects of the vast Christian tradition must be communicated for there to be an authentic Christian community? Do we bring all the details of canon law and liturgical law? Do we bring a westernized form of Christianity, or do we more simply bring the gospel and let the Christian faith evolve and develop at its own pace? There are no simple answers to these questions, and yet we must make some response.

First, we can remind ourselves that there is, according to Vatican II, a hierarchy of truths. In the Decree on Ecumenism, we read that "when comparing doctrines with one another, we should remember that in Catholic doctrine there exists an order of 'hierarchy' of truths, since they vary in their relation to the foundation of Christian faith" (no. 11).[10] While the document goes on to speak briefly of the triune God and of Jesus Christ the redeemer, it is noteworthy that it does not further specify or define what this hierarchy of truths consists of. That there is a hierarchy is important in itself, though, and quite different from the view of Pius XI in *Mortalium Animos* (1928) where he speaks of the assent due to *all* truths, without making any distinction between central and less central truths of the Christian faith.

To assist with this thorny problem of the center of Christian faith, some scholars have suggested the advisability of creating short, summary formulas of the Christian faith.[11] They envision a pastoral effort to present the essential content of Christian faith in a form simplified enough so that it appears understandable, conformable with experience, and personally inviting. These short formulas would carry significance in the areas of ecumenism, catechesis, and inculturation. In each area one is trying to share the faith with others, and trying to do this with some reflective understanding of what is essential and what is less important. On the one hand, the short formula can result in reductionism or a diluting of faith, the loss of the richness of the tradition. On the other hand it does prevent overloading the neophyte and helps one not to confuse essentials and accidentals. The short formula thus both reduces and concentrates the faith.

Another way of dealing with the problem of the core or kernel is by reflecting on two approaches we have to understanding reality, namely the classical approach and a more historical approach. When using the classical approach, we speak of essences, essentials and accidentals; we posit universals that are true always and everywhere and stress the unchanging nature of truth. Yet even if we are inclined to this way of thinking, we still have to answer the difficult question of what the essence of Christian faith is and what are the accidentals. The line between the two is not sharp and clear.

With a more historical, empirical understanding of reality, we are struck by the changes that occur in the flow of time, and by the diversity between cultures and peoples in the present. We realize that truth must be reformulated and reexpressed as it is learned and lived in different cultural contexts. We are much more skeptical about getting to the essence of anything, skeptical about the unchanging, or universal, absolute nature of truth.

What is the way forward? Perhaps the best way to proceed is to think of Christianity as a series of concentric circles, with the more important content at the center and the less important at the periphery. What exactly is at the center remains somewhat undefined, or rather is actually continually being refined and reformulated, depending on the situation and context. Karl Rahner, when asked how he would identify the center of his theology, replied: "That's hard to say. The center of my theology? Good Lord, that can't be anything else but God as mystery and Jesus Christ, the crucified and risen One, as the historical event in which this God turns irreversibly towards us in self-communication. So, in principle, you can't name just *one* center."[12]

In inculturating gospel values, therefore, one must always turn to the center, to Jesus Christ, his life and message. Thus one turns to the four gospels more than to the letter to the Thessalonians, to Jesus rather than to St. Jude, to the central virtues of love and justice, to the central sacraments of baptism and eucharist. Christianity is to be viewed not as a book or series of teachings, but as a way of life, the life of Christ lived in our day and age under the inspiration of the Spirit. An attitude of trust becomes essential, trust in the Spirit promised by Jesus who will guide us to the fullness of truth, trust in the Spirit already at work in those we minister to and with. All Christians from the pope to the newly baptized are disciples or learners. We are all in the process of becoming Christian. We all fall short of appreciating, understanding, and living the full mystery of God's love in Christ Jesus.

Perhaps the best way to conclude this chapter on the theological bases for inculturation is to remind ourselves that the fullness of truth is ahead of us. We are a pilgrim, searching people. The mission of inculturation is one key part of that search for the fullness of Christ, a fullness that will only come at the end. In the present we should try to appreciate and rejoice in the many myriad ways in which different communities of Christians, old and new communities, African and American communities, point to and reflect the unfathomable richness of the mystery of Christ.

5. The How of Inculturation

From this brief review of the meaning and history of inculturation and the examination of some of its theological underpinnings, we move to the more difficult and more practical question of the *how* of inculturation. The question of method is difficult but very important. In a sense it is a bit artificial to step back from actually doing theology or inculturation to inquire how it is or should be done. And yet the problem of method remains crucial if one is to carefully, faithfully, and competently begin the process of inculturation.

In describing a method for inculturation, I am in reality delineating a method for all Christian ministry, since I believe that all ministry involves the principles and attitudes of inculturation. Wherever one is, one tries to stir up the gospel values that are already present and bring to bear the gospel values that are absent.[1]

I will begin by suggesting a number of different situations that can all be classified under ministry, situations where inculturation of gospel values is called for. Second, using the diagram of a circle, I will set forth the basic elements involved in each situation. Third, I will expand each of the three poles of the circle and describe the interaction among them.

The most obvious example of a situation calling for inculturation would be that of a *missionary* beginning a new assignment in East Africa. But the following situations also involve inculturation: the *priest* in the rectory preparing his sermon for the coming Sunday and reflecting on how God's word might both challenge and strengthen his particular congregation, a *bishop or group of bishops* writing a pastoral letter to their dioceses on justice or the evils of racism, a *director of religious education* beginning an assignment in a parish where a number of minority groups are represented, a *layperson* advising a friend or relative on choosing a career or vocation, a *theologian* writing an essay on the meaning of Sunday worship for the Christian community, a *retreat director* guiding a person through a weekend or five day retreat, and finally a *pastoral assistant* (religious or lay) in a parish trying to reconcile a husband and wife after a prolonged and heated argument.

These situations vary with respect to the identity of the minister (from layperson to bishop), with respect to location (from first world to third world), and with respect to outcome (from a preached sermon to a written essay to addressing a local situation of need). In spite of such differences there are elements common to all eight situations, in addition to a basic common method that can be followed in facing each of them. If we can gain insight into this method and into the attitudes required to carry it out, we will move forward in clarifying what inculturation is all about and how it is accomplished.

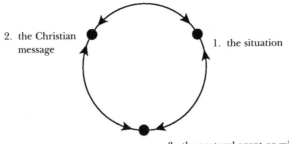

2. the Christian message

1. the situation

3. the pastoral agent or minister

This diagram presents what I call the pastoral, or hermeneutical, circle. Its three poles indicate the major elements in each of the seven situations. The arrows between the poles indicate that movement around the circle must proceed in both clockwise and counterclockwise directions. The first pole represents the given situation, which eventually means persons in need and in search of God's word and will. The second pole represents the Christian message, the insight and input from scripture, tradition, and Christian life that serves to illuminate and guide the present situation. The third pole refers to the pastoral agent, minister, or agent of inculturation who tries to mediate God's word (pole 2) to the particular situation (pole 1).

As is by now perhaps apparent, we are echoing Paul Tillich's method of correlation, whereby the Christian message with its answers is brought to bear on the human situation with its questions.[2] In his terminology, this is a process of correlating situation and message, or question and answer. For purposes of clarification, and to show the importance of the agent of inculturation, we have added the agent as the third pole of the pastoral circle. Our point in employing this diagram is to present a pedagogical tool that will assist the person involved in inculturation to become more aware of how he or she actually has ministered and should minister in particular situations.

While each of the eight situations could be examined more carefully in light of the diagram, it seems better to stay with the general features. In the next few pages, therefore, we will explain more fully the three poles of the circle and how the interaction among them occurs.

The Situation (Pole 1)

This pole of the circle stands for the setting in which and for which the agent of inculturation becomes active. In the final analysis the situation consists of persons. All theology, ministry, and inculturation is in service to human needs. There is some problem, tension, question, new possibility, or opportunity that calls for reflection, response, resolution, or decision. As we would not need medical doctors if we all enjoyed perfect health, so there would be no need for agents of inculturation if we all lived gospel values fully.

Every pastoral situation is always under the influence of sin and grace, good and evil. There are positive and negative values in every situation, problems and yet possibilities. The positive values or possibilities become the stepping stones for pastoral action because they represent in theological terms the *semina verbi,* the seeds of the word that must be tapped.

Thus the first task of the agent of inculturation is to become acquainted with the situation in terms of factual data as well as values present or absent. This means beginning with the real rather than the ideal or idealized situation. The myths, dreams, idols, ultimate concerns, and world view of those involved must be uncovered in a process that calls for careful study and patient listening. Depending on the type and complexity of the situation, various disciplines can be turned to for assistance, including history, anthropology, sociology, and economics. These disciplines help us to read a particular situation, to understand its problems, and to spark the beginnings of a solution. The humanities, art, and literature also help to illuminate the situation.

Cultural anthropology would obviously be most helpful in contributing to an understanding of situations where in-culturation must take place.[3] The study of traditional rituals and festive celebrations, for example, provides insight into the values, ways of relating, and ways of thinking of a partic-ular culture. Ideally the particular situation or culture should be studied diachronically and synchronically. The diachronic dimension means that the historical developments and events, the key moments and persons in the history of a particular culture or situation should be examined. The synchronic dimension means that the particular situation in question should be compared with other contemporary situations. The diachronic dimension looks back in time, while the synchronic looks out in space, in the present, to gain insights that add to an understanding of specific cultural situations.

This analysis cannot be done exclusively by the agent of inculturation, but should always involve self-analysis on the part of those in the situation, too. The pastoral agent helps those in the situation to name their own hopes and fears, their sinful and graced moments. The situation must be examined in its temporal and spatial dimensions, for no situation is completely isolated or without a history.

Unless the situation is adequately understood, the pastoral action and direction will be inadequate. The result will be what Tillich said is the difficulty with most sermons, that they give answers to questions no one is asking. The actual, specific situation and its needs are not addressed, and so the supposed solution avoids or bypasses the nub or kernel of the problematic situation.

Inculturation insists on the importance of analyzing the situation. It also reminds us of the complexity and difficulty of the analysis. In truth, no analysis is ever complete, since situations are changing and cultures are evolving. Yet if we are to inculturate gospel values into situations and uncover values already present, then familiarity with the situation is essential.

The Christian Message (Pole 2)

While attention to the first pole of the circle ensures that the present situation is understood and addressed, attention to the second pole ensures that Christian values are brought to bear on that situation. A pastoral strategy is formed that accords with God's word and truth, especially as focused in the life and message of Jesus Christ. This is done by examining the myriad ways in which God has spoken and acted in human history: through scripture, tradition, and contemporary embodiments and manifestations of the word of God.

The Christian message involves the entirety of the Christian heritage, our common Christian memory, which acts as a source and resource for the present, offering parallels, case studies, and the wisdom of the past. For the Christian agent of inculturation, the Christian message centers on the word of God in scripture, especially on the life, teaching, death, and resurrection of Jesus Christ. The minister must have a critical understanding of, and working familiarity with, the scriptures so that he or she can lead others into them as a resource.

Although the scriptures may be the definitive and normative word of God, they are not the final word in the temporal sense. They are the all-important beginning of the Christian tradition, but the past and present life of the Christian community also functions as part of the Christian message. Included here would be church councils and creeds, the writings of theologians, the lives and writings of saints, and the liturgical traditions of the church. Finally, the writings of contemporary theologians and Christians must be heeded in bringing the Christian message to bear on a particular situation. One reads and interprets the Christian message from one's own particular tradition, whether that is Roman Catholic or another tradition.

Two difficult questions arise in this process, questions that demand far more reflection than we can give in this handbook. First is the question of the relative weight or normativity of the varied expressions of the Christian message such as scripture, tradition, magisterial pronouncements, the consensus of the faithful, and opinions of theologians. Obviously scripture remains the abiding norm, the perennial source of life and truth. But this norm must be studied and understood in light of the tradition of interpretation by the church through its magisterium as well as its theologians and biblical scholars. And as we have seen, we must be open to the present revelation of God in and through the signs of the times. In addition, we are a prophetic people, and the God who spoke through the prophets continues to speak today. Thus the desire to know exactly what the Christian message is for a particular situation requires much study, dialogue, and prayer.

The second question is whether there is an unchanging and unchangeable kernel or center of the Christian message, and, if so, what it consists of? We have already mentioned this second problem in treating the history and meaning of inculturation. While there may not be agreement on the precise nature of the center or kernel of the Christian message, or agreement on the hierarchy of truths, we cannot embark on the process of inculturation without some reflection on this difficult question. Otherwise we risk substituting and perhaps imposing accidentals, rather than moving to the center and substance of the Christian faith.

The result of attending to the second pole of the pastoral circle is that the situation is not seen in isolation, but in continuity with God's word in the past and in similar present situations. The strength and insight, the comfort and challenge of God's word is brought to bear on the present situation. In this way the Christian community grows and advances into the future through the constant retrieval of the riches of its tradition.

The Agent of Inculturation or Minister of the Gospel (Pole 3)

The third pole refers to the resource person, the minister, or the agent who has the mission and task of inculturation. In addition to knowing the situation and the Christian message, the agent of inculturation should also be aware of his or her own strengths and weaknesses, biases and prejudices. We all have filters through which we experience reality and judge situations. These filters may, for example, be North American, male, or middle class, all of which influence the way we think and act. The pastoral agent should also be aware of his or her vision of church, gospel, theology, and tradition so that he or she can share this with others, letting it be modified and developed in that interchange. Some persons have specific skills for listening, others for leadership, and the more aware we are of our own abilities and lacks, the better we can carry out the process of inculturation.

Because of the limited nature of our talents and abilities, because of the complexity of the issues involved, because the agent of inculturation may remain to some extent an outsider to the culture, there is a special need for teamwork and collaboration. The agent of inculturation is not the sole resource or the sole leader, but is perhaps best seen as the one who works with others, who complements his or her own talents and resources with the talents of others. Through community effort we are much more likely to achieve solutions that are more helpful and more lasting, because so much more collaborative input has gone into the formulation not only of the solution but also of the problem.[4]

Thus the agent of inculturation acts as a facilitator, not to make decisions for others as much as to offer perspectives and resources so that those in the situation make their own informed decisions. This ministry/facilitation involves a dialogical stance, allowing those in the situation to explore their own values, goals, visions, and options. The final strategy, the pastoral action, must arise from the situation and those in it, and not be one imposed from above or from outside. It will always remain difficult for the pastoral agent to achieve that delicate balance between necessary involvement in the situation (walking in their shoes) and the outside, critical perspective that is also needed. It is a continuing struggle to maintain the balance between immersion and empathy on the one hand, and critical conviction and assertiveness on the other.

The agent of inculturation must become a trusted authority and resource for those in the cultural situation. The ministry of inculturation means serving, putting the needs of the situation before one's own agenda. The agent of inculturation enters the situation with respect and humility, knowing that he or she treads on holy ground and at the invitation of those concerned. He or she comes with the conviction that God is already present in the situation. The task of the facilitator is to let the power and love of God more deeply illuminate and guide that context or culture.

Among the many attitudes or dispositions needed by the agent of inculturation are the following. One must be patient, since the acceptance of gospel values depends on human freedom and the grace of God. One must be ready and willing to face failure or rejection. In the ongoing, new, and creative process of inculturation, mistakes may be made, and as one moves ahead, one can only hope to learn from those mistakes. At the same time that one ministers as an agent of inculturation, one must let oneself be ministered to. And in addition to offering resources as a teacher, one must be willing to learn. It is this last point that makes the process of inculturation so exciting, for in the process of sharing and giving, one receives some portion of the hundredfold. One's own faith is deepened and one's vision broadened. Above all, one needs a listening heart—an ability to listen to the call of God as it comes through the tradition, and, equally important, an ability to listen to the call of God as it comes through the persons in the situation where one is ministering. This listening attitude stems from a humility, demands an asceticism, and presupposes a deep love and respect for those with whom one works and ministers. More than any other word, listening seems to me to be the key to the successful practice of inculturation.[5]

Interaction of the Three Poles

With the three poles of the circle more clearly understood, we can explain more fully how movement occurs among the poles. By using the device of a closed circle, we indicate that movement must come full circle. The starting point is not as important as the fact that one completes the circle, touching all three poles. While at a given moment there may be a concentration on either the message or the cultural situation, eventually these intensive moments must be complemented by relational moves to the other two poles.

All three poles must be involved to ensure that the pastoral action is Christian, that it is appropriate and fitting, and that it draws on competent expertise. Movement proceeds in both clockwise and counterclockwise directions; it is a two way street. Thus the situation effects what we look for in the tradition, and the tradition in turn addresses questions to the situation. In the process of making the resources of the Christian message apply to a situation, we enlarge our understanding and appreciation of the message itself. Two examples of this enlargement would be the new insight we have gained into the scriptural message concerning the poor and concerning women. Liberation theology forces us to examine more carefully the extent to which God is on the side of the poor and the wealthy come under God's judgment. Feminist theology enables us to see more clearly the central role of women during the passion and death of Jesus Christ, and hence also in the awakening of faith in Jesus and his proclamation as risen Lord.

We might therefore consider the pastoral circle not so much as a closed circle but as a spiral, with movement around the spiral in ascending fashion. That is to say, when each of the poles has been involved and decisions made and actions taken, the circle begins anew. In this way movement around the pastoral circle becomes an ongoing learning process, with ever-new interpretations of the Christian message being brought to bear on contexts that are themselves changing as well as being seen with new insight. The gospel is never fully inculturated, therefore, for it is always possible to make our lives and our communities approximate more closely the life and message of Jesus Christ.

How does one describe the interaction among the three poles? We would suggest the image of a conversation among three partners, all of whom are searching for the truth. The truth emerges from the dynamic interaction or conversation among them. It emerges when the values and goals of the three poles mutually confirm, challenge, and corroborate each other. The word *resonance* describes the moment of truth, when the three separate poles merge in mutual illumination and the mind rests in a truth that is shared by the three partners.

It must be noted that though the final decision on pastoral action is one made in peace and directed toward peace, the process itself is not always so peaceful. Scripture, for example, must sometimes function as a prophetic word, a two-edged sword. The pastoral agent of inculturation must sometimes be prophetic and critical. The situation or culture, in turn, challenges the Christian message and occasionally contemporary church teaching to put the spirit of the law over its letter. The situation also reminds us that the Spirit who spoke in the past also speaks today in exciting new ways in light of the specific needs of that context. Only through such interaction will gospel values be contextualized or inculturated in the modern world with its variety of settings and cultures.

Further Reflections and Implications

The use of the circle to depict the process of contextualization points to the difficulty of building a community that is both Christian and true to its own cultural heritage. On the one hand, the local community cannot be so Roman or Romanized that it sees itself simply as a carbon copy of the European church, a church exported around the world. On the other hand, it cannot be closed to input from and connections with the larger community in space and in time. Increasingly no community is an island unto itself. Every local Christian community must maintain its links with other communities in the present around the world, and with communities of the past, through an understanding of Christian tradition.

The circle also points to the need for the agent of inculturation—whether bishop, priest, or lay person—to be a facilitator and not an intruder. He or she must be a person of faith and compassion, able to listen and to learn. Instead of simply repeating the ways and answers of the past, he or she must enter creatively into the new present, enabling

God's word and the Christian message to come alive both as comfort and as challenge. The agent or leader cannot do this alone; the community itself must be involved, and he or she serves to gather them and bring forth the gifts, viewpoints, and experiences of God and Christ already present in that community.

The circle, and the entire project of inculturation or contextualization, only makes sense in light of a deep, faith-filled understanding of incarnation and grace. That is to say, the word and power of God, which was definitively present in Jesus Christ, remains present and available in the world today in every cultural situation. The mission of the church includes the creative task of correlating the Christian message with ever-new situations. In this way gospel values become inculturated or localized. Inculturation is achieved not by importing grace from outside, as if it were not already available in the situation, but by stirring up the grace of God that has already been decisively offered through Jesus Christ. The Christian agent of inculturation does not minister in a world untouched by God's loving grace, nor does he or she enter into any situation that is beyond hope. Rather, he or she brings to life the seeds that have already been planted by the universal saving power of God.

Much more could be said about the difficult process of analyzing complex cultural situations, about the relation between reflection and action, and about the continual evaluation of the results of pastoral actions. Because I have focused on method, I have remained rather general and abstract, but I have tried to provide a framework for carrying on the work of inculturation. In the next chapters I will illustrate how this process is initiated in different cultural settings, namely Nigeria, Latin America, and the United States.

6. Toward Inculturation in Nigeria

Through the image of the pastoral circle, the previous chapter outlined a general method for the process of inculturation. It described the various elements and interactions that must be present and attended to if theology is to become localized or contextualized, if gospel values are to become rooted in a particular situation. In this chapter we will begin to employ the pastoral circle with the situation of Nigeria in mind. Why Nigeria? Any place in Africa could have been chosen, for there especially the question of inculturation is being raised. I choose Nigeria because that is the area I am most familiar with after five years of teaching and parish work in Port Harcourt, Nigeria. In addition, Nigeria is the giant of Africa, with a population estimated to be one hundred million; one out of every four Africans is Nigerian. One projection indicates that by the year 2050 Nigeria will be the fourth largest nation in the world, with over four hundred million persons. The church is growing rapidly there, and it offers an interesting test case for the process and reality of inculturation.

We are moving from the general method to the more specific use of that method in a particular context. It must be stated clearly, however, that we are in reality not yet engaged in actual inculturation. Why? First, we are speaking broadly about Nigerian culture and church, which must eventually be made more specific in terms of a local church or community. Second, we are writing about inculturation, and actual inculturation is not something done in schools, libraries, or laboratories (even if these are essential for the overall process of inculturation) but in the local situation with the local community or church. Third, I myself am not a Nigerian, but an outsider, and at best I can only assist in the process of inculturation by collaborating with and encouraging Nigerians—insiders—to undertake and carry it out. In spite of these cautions and limitations, it does seem valuable to show in a general way how one begins to think about and to plan the process of inculturation with Nigeria in mind.[1]

Cultural Values and Disvalues

The process of inculturation, as we saw in the previous chapter, involves continual movement around the pastoral circle: analysis of the cultural situation, examination of the biblical message and church tradition, and reflection on one's own experience.

We will begin here by analyzing the cultural situation, which was referred to as the first pole of the pastoral circle. Our goal is to highlight those elements of the culture that are of special positive or negative significance for Christian theology. Here again we must admit our limitations. The insights of a professional anthropologist, of a sociologist or ethnographer, and of an historian of religions would be most valuable. My own approach is more modest—to draw on the writings of others and on personal experience, and to set forth particular values and disvalues of Nigerian culture. Obviously I am making generalizations that will not fit every subculture and ethnic grouping of Nigeria, but on the other hand much of what I say will be applicable not only to Nigeria but to other parts of West Africa.

The values and disvalues discussed below have been chosen with respect to their implications for the process of inculturation. In a later section of this chapter I will begin correlating Nigerian values and disvalues with biblical,

Christian values. I am focusing on the present, and here too admit limitations. To truly understand the present, one must have a sense of history, of how the present with its values and disvalues emerged from the past. The study of the history of Nigerian culture and cultures is thus important, but it falls outside the scope of this modest undertaking.

Familial solidarity. "The isolated self is an abstraction, it is unreal." One quickly senses and feels the truth of this statement in Nigerian culture. One is identified by one's family, which is the extended family, often including aunts and uncles, cousins, in-laws, nieces, and nephews. Extended also over time, the family is continually linked with those who have gone before. Here one notes the respect and reverence shown to ancestors, particularly to parents, grandparents, and great-grandparents who have died. These ancestors remain present in memory and imagination; they watch over and serve as examples to the present generation. There is deep communion between the living and the dead.

Children too are precious; not to have children is the exception and is often seen as a disgrace. For it is the children who care for the parents in their old age, who pass on the family name to future generations. The elders of a family receive special dignity by virtue of their age, wisdom, and experience. They are honored and consulted on key questions.

Loyalty to and support for one's family are primary. One is one's brother's and sister's keeper. A key image of sin is separation, isolation from family, and breaking the familial solidarity. One always remembers and returns to one's roots insofar as possible, even if one has moved to a different location. Thus at Christmas, for example, those living in the cities return to the villages, to be reunited with their extended family, especially their parents, and to reestablish contact with their roots.

Sense of ritual and festivity. A celebration without song and dance, without a deliberate, unrushed atmosphere, is no celebration at all. When Nigerians gather to celebrate, as they frequently do, the occasion is most often marked by joy and festivity. Traditional dances with traditional costumes link the present with the past, and unite the entire community in a shared ritual. The sacred and the secular intertwine; the formal dance of those in costume invites the active participation of the onlookers. The formal presentations at a formal banquet go together with a long and unhurried time spent together in friendly joking and conversation. While there are occasions for elaborate, stylized ritual and traditional dance and music, more spontaneous song and dance also have a time and place.

Depending on the nature of the occasion, children and infants are present, drawn lovingly into the richness of the culture and its traditions. One cannot, one does not, celebrate alone; one does not truly celebrate without song and dance.

Sense of the sacred. No sharp distinction, and certainly no separation, is made between the sacred and the secular. The divine influence is felt continually, in all times and places, and not simply on holy days such as Sunday, or in holy places such as shrines. Truly we are never far from the divine and its various manifestations in the world of spirits. The world is God's creation, and God still remains present and watchful over creation. Hence the sacredness of creation, in which religion has to do with all of one's life and activity and cannot be separated out or compartmentalized. Life itself, the gift of God, is intensively and pervasively religious—played out in the presence of, and in contact with, the divine. A theology of the death of God makes no sense in this context, and is simply a laughing matter.

Primacy of the personal. Before one goes about one's business with another person, one must first greet that person and show respect by establishing the more personal relationship. Regardless of how one feels, the personal greeting always comes at the beginning and conclusion of an encounter, even on the most mundane business level. The personal thus takes priority over the impersonal. Efficiency and getting the job done are not the only values, and indeed not the highest values. In place of task orientation is the more leisurely way of developing a sense of familiarity and friendship before one gets on with the business at hand, to use a non-Nigerian expression.

This primacy of the personal also means that mechanical explanations of events are often seen as insufficient. In place of chance or accidental happenings, one usually searches for some personal causality behind events.

There is value in being together, in spending time with friends and acquaintances. Time spent in conversation is not idle time but an opportunity to share, to appreciate each other, and to grow in wisdom and humanity. The marketplace manifests this primacy of the personal in several ways. One goes there to shop but also to meet and be with friends. One does not rush the shopping, but walks about, looks, and talks. And in the actual purchasing, there is normally dialogue, haggling, and bargaining over the final price instead of the more impersonal tag with a fixed price.

The mother with her child nestled on her back, who works in the fields or the marketplace, and the eight year old sister who takes care of her little brother for hours on end reveal this priority of the personal. Personal attention and contact, so important in the life and development of the child, take the place of baby carriages.

Hospitality. Another example of the primacy of the personal is the attitude of open and generous hospitality to strangers and guests. One readily and graciously welcomes guests into one's home, and shares what one has, whether great or small. "If there is food enough for three, there is enough for five or six." In situations where telephones are non-existent, or communications are often unreliable, one welcomes with joy and charity the unexpected, surprise guest. Indeed, there is a sense of the sacred in the coming of a guest, a sense that the divine is calling on us: that truly love of neighbor, love for the stranger and the guest, is inseparable from love of God.

Life. Perhaps the most central value that one observes in Nigeria is the wonderful respect for and love of life. This may sound vague and general, and of course it can become so, but in the Nigerian context it takes on a variety of shapes and forms, or concrete manifestations. One lives close to life; one lives close to death, and hence gains a deeper appreciation for life. The elderly remain at home as long as possible, rather than being sent to special nursing homes or hospitals. Sickness and dying are not usually faced in hospitals but in homes and villages, with the comforting presence of family, neighbors, and relatives.

Children are the most visible signs of hope, signs of life, and in Nigeria children are omnipresent. Children renew the life of us all, reminding us of the child in us, the joy, the hope, the potential, the dreams that still lie before us. Precisely because of the simplicity of life (less mechanized, less automated, less thing-oriented, less material), life itself, our common sharing in something much greater than ourselves, is appreciated and celebrated.

Thus far in our examination of the first pole of the pastoral circle, namely the situation or context, we have examined some of the positive values in Nigerian culture. In addition to the positive, however, one must look also at the negative side, for not only is grace and truth present in all cultural contexts, but also sin and evil or evil tendencies.

Often the very values that are positive are linked with disvalues, if the positive value is exaggerated or taken to an extreme. Let us now look briefly at the negative side, the disvalues of Nigerian culture.

Disvalues. Familial solidarity creates strong social, economic and religious bonds. But the strength of family ties can also be turned in on itself, so that the outsider receives no justice and no compassion. While providing for the welfare of close relatives and friends, one refuses to see beyond the family and to work sufficiently for the good of the state or nation. Tribalism with all of its ambiguity is an example of this. If tribalism results in hostility or indifference to those in other ethnic groups, then it has taken a turn for the worse and will prevent the emergence of true nationalism or internationalism.

The love of children, and the desire to have children, is beautiful. But if it is so imperative that the man or woman who cannot have children is held in disgrace, then it has gone too far. The worth of a woman cannot simply be judged by her ability to bear children. When absolutized, this value becomes a disvalue.

Personalism, the emphasis on personal rather than impersonal values, has a key contribution to make. But if it means loyalty to one's friends at any price, and at the expense of the common good and the law of the nation, then it has become a disvalue.

Finally, one can speak of the danger of greed. So much is happening in Nigeria—new ideas, new products, new possibilities. Television opens up new horizons, and everyone wants a share of the pie, of the new good life. The new attitude of consumerism needs careful scrutiny and criticism, for it threatens to undermine the stability, the sense of cooperation and the sense of solidarity that has been a hallmark of the culture.

The list could be lengthened, and a much more nuanced and careful study of the values and disvalues of Nigerian culture remains an ongoing task in the process of inculturation. As one studies any culture, one becomes aware of ambiguities in that culture—the complex mixing of good and evil, of positive and negative possibilities. Urban conditions exemplify such ambiguity in Nigeria. In Lagos, for example, there is beauty and squalor, well-paid employment and far too common unemployment. There are places of recreation, as well as overcrowded streets and houses. There is wealth and poverty, hunger and feasting. There are modern medical facilities, but these are far from adequate. Nigeria's cities remain ambiguous. They are signs of hope, of a new future, but also signs of despair, of overpopulation, of the loss of personal roots.

The oil boom is another striking example of ambiguity. The promised new Nigeria remains far from a reality, and one hears of oil doom rather than boom. The new wealth has made a difference, but not all to the good. The rich and powerful become richer and more powerful, while the mass of citizens see the better life eluding them, appearing only on television and in newspapers but not in their villages and homes. Oil money has been used not for the good of the entire nation, for lasting progress, but for the benefit of the few, for short-term gains, and for show.

Symbols of change. As one examines the Nigerian situation, one is made aware of tremendous change. Nigeria is trying to do in forty years what it took Europe and the United States one hundred and forty years to do. The rapid changes produced by this effort have resulted in gaps and tensions between cities and villages, old and young, rich and poor, the educated and the illiterate, and the modern and the traditional. Four symbols that point to the nature of these changes are the wrist watch, the pen, the portable radio, and the coin and paper money. The wrist watch means scheduling rather than more personal and leisurely ways of interacting. We can become enslaved to time and efficiency. The pen stands for literacy, for the world of education and books, which is so different from the oral culture of years gone by. The portable radio brings the news, the values and disvalues of the world to the smallest village. It opens up vast horizons and reminds us that in one sense the world is now a global village. Finally, paper money and the coin represent the economy, which is now international. The local market is linked to the world market, and fixed prices have become more and more common, replacing the custom of bargaining over prices.

Culture texts. Examination of the values and disvalues of a cultural situation demands immersion in and familiarity with that situation. But what parts, events, or aspects of the situation does one examine? Anthropologists can help us with their study of culture. One school of anthropologists speaks of the examination of "culture texts." "Texts" mean not only written texts but also places, events, ways of interacting, and rituals that reveal key characteristics of a culture.[2]

A few examples of culture texts from Nigeria that reveal values and disvalues in the culture are the marketplace, the advent of the supermarket, the mission school, annual religious and agricultural festivals, a television show that has achieved great popularity, the annual celebration of Independence Day, the ever-present roadblocks, the content and use of proverbs in public discourse, the traditional healer, the kola nut, the village meeting place, marriage arrangements and rituals, burial rites, traditional naming ceremonies, the installation of a new chief or leader, traditional rites of passage, the mushrooming independent Christian churches, airports, and the telephone. Examining any one of these realities in depth and detail, to see how it operates, who is in charge, who is excluded, how it relates to other aspects of Nigerian life, and how it has changed or developed in recent years, would enable one to enter rather deeply into the culture of Nigeria, and thereby into the process of inculturation.

Areas and Examples of Inculturation

A whole range of areas of church life calls for inculturation. Among these, we will comment on the following: catechesis, liturgy and sacraments, church art and architecture, church structure, the mission of the church, prayer and spirituality, and Christian theology. All of these are areas where the process of inculturation must take place, and where Christian gospel values should influence and mold behavior. In keeping with the nature of our inquiry and the limits of this introductory handbook, we will raise more questions than we can answer.

One complicating factor, already noted but worth repeating because of its importance, is that for the most part in Nigeria we are not taking the gospel to where it has never been preached. Rather we are involved in places where Christianity has been established, where missionaries from Europe or America have planted the faith. In other words, the gospel has already been brought, the liturgy has been celebrated, and catechism has been learned. Naturally this was done from the perspective of the different missionaries, whether they were Irish or Dutch, American or Italian. So it is much more difficult to distinguish what is European Catholicism from what is essential to Catholicism and Christianity wherever it is. In other words, we must sometimes free the present form of Catholicism from its particular European analogue, in order to encourage and foster a new creative inculturation with African values and thought patterns.

Catechesis. The numbers of young children attending catechism classes faithfully throughout Nigeria is astounding. Much catechesis is geared to children preparing for first communion or for confirmation. And this will continue to be the case. But what catechisms are being used? Do they reflect African ways of thinking and learning, or are they simply imported from Europe or America? Should there be more inclusion of proverbs and stories in catechesis, both of which feature prominently in African life as well as in the life and ministry of Jesus? As a matter of fact, the wisdom literature of the Hebrew scriptures, especially the book of Proverbs, is very popular throughout Africa. In a sense, African Christian theology should develop its own book of proverbs, proverbs that are deeply rooted in African religious tradition and imagery. More effort should be given to adult catechesis, so that adults working in schools, the marketplace, and the business world can inculturate Christian values into those spheres. There is great love for the Bible in Nigeria among Catholics and Protestants. How can Bible study be more central to catechesis for everyone, and not only for those involved in Bible instructors' groups?[3]

In a letter on ministries in the church, Pope Paul VI suggested the creation of new official ministries and named as one possibility the ministry of catechist.[4] This role is extremely important in the rapidly growing church of Nigeria. Yet insufficient recognition—and training—is given to the thousands of catechists. Should the church, the parish, and the diocese not give more official status to the role of catechist and consider the suggestion of Paul VI to make it one of the official ministries of the church, with appropriate training followed by a public liturgical celebration when the catechists are installed?

Vatican II called for the renewal of the catechumenate. At St. Joseph's Parish in Benin City, Nigeria, during the 1988 Easter vigil celebration, three hundred and sixty-eight *adults* were baptized. Approximately two hundred of these chose baptism by immersion. Another six hundred adults are already signed up for the next catechumenate program. They will enter the program based on the new Rite of Christian Initiation of Adults (RCIA). Some have called this the most mature and creative theological-liturgical document to result from the reforms of Vatican II. How is this document being implemented in parishes in Nigeria? The document calls for a lengthy, creative process of initiation for adults or fallen-away Catholics. The initiation process is itself a model of inculturation, of how adult Catholics are to be inculturated into the Christian community. It involves catechesis, liturgical celebrations, group meetings, individual sponsors, and apostolic experiences; creative adaptation in its implementation is called for. I believe that this new rite offers tremendous possibilities for inculturation. If it is implemented properly it will go far toward forming mature, adult Christians who will then have the proper attitudes and resources for collaborating and contributing in the overall process of inculturation.

Art and architecture. One senses a tremendous gap between traditional African art and the art and statues of most Catholic churches. Instead of coming from the local soil, much church art has been imported from Europe; thus the local crucifix likely depicts the Jesus Christ of Ireland or Germany, and the Sacred Heart is a drawing from Italy or America. The value of this should not be overlooked, the reminder that the Catholic faith is universal. But a greater disvalue also surfaces, namely that indigenous artists are not invited to share their faithful insight and imagination. The result is that Christianity remains somewhat foreign to Nigerian art and culture. So too with music: although Gregorian chant has its rightful place in binding us to a long tradition and to the universality of the church, it should be complemented by music that is more in tune with the African soul. Likewise, the latest liturgical music from the United States or Europe should not simply be imported or transported, but rather should serve to encourage the creativity of Nigerian musicians. Music in Nigeria is usually connected with dance. Nigerian music calls forth not only the voice but the whole person to expression and movement. While this connection is evident in varying degrees in the Nigerian church, surely it can and should develop much further. The sources for creativity in liturgical music in Nigeria are barely being touched.

With the widespread building of new churches and the expansion of old churches, architecture is basically simple and functional. Yet questions should be raised about the design of church buildings and how they encourage enriched liturgical celebrations. Is there room for movement, for processions in and around the church? Must the long and narrow church, with those in the back far distant from the altar, be the normal pattern? Are altar rails that falsely separate the sanctuary from the pews necessary? Are pews called for, or perhaps other forms of seating that allow more interaction among the participants? An opportunity is present because there is so much building in progress. And yet so much art and architecture seem to be imitative, importation, rather than a creative, indigenous rethinking of what a church building should be and how it should function in the Nigerian village or city in accord with Nigerian patterns of meeting and celebration.

Christology. In the remainder of this chapter I will briefly examine several key areas of Christian theology to see how the thrust toward inculturation will both challenge those areas and offer them new possibilities. From the whole spectrum of theology and doctrine, we will focus on six areas, beginning with christology.[5]

From Latin America, in light of the massive presence of poverty and oppression there, we hear much of Jesus Christ the liberator. He impels the Christian community to work for liberation from sin, injustice, and oppression. This is an example of inculturation in that particular church context. Something similar must be done for Nigeria and Africa. Obviously some elements of liberation are needed in Nigeria. Yet other cultural and religious elements in Africa have much to contribute to the development of an African christology.

Should Jesus Christ not be preached as the one who liberates or saves from the power of evil, which in Nigeria is often felt to be the power of evil spirits? Jesus Christ has triumphed over Satan, and Christians now share in that victory. According to Romans 8, nothing—no evil spirit, no wicked forces—can separate us from the love of God in Christ Jesus.

In a society characterized by strong ties with and respect for ancestors, should we not emphasize with Saint Paul that Jesus Christ was the first to rise from the dead and hence can be considered our proto-ancestor? Giving Jesus the title *ancestor* fits in very well with African understanding. It means that he is for us an elder in the community, an intercessor or mediator between God and humanity, one who guards and protects the human community.

Jesus Christ came not to be served, but to serve. His style of leadership, in contrast to that of the pagans, was servant leadership. How this relates to traditional rulership in Nigeria, to the ways that chiefs and elders interact with their people, must be explored. Especially in Nigeria today, with the transition from a traditional to a modernized society, when traditional modes of leadership are under pressure and consumerism is in the ascendancy, it seems crucial to let the image of Jesus the servant exert more influence in Catholic theology and ministry.

Similarly, there should be much more emphasis on Jesus Christ the healer. This aspect of Jesus is not new but is at the heart of the New Testament. What Nigeria must do is let this message become a reality through preaching and teaching, through sacraments and sacramentals, through prayer and petition.

In these and in many other ways, the Nigerian church will begin to take more seriously the challenge issued by Pope John Paul II in 1980 on his visit to Africa. In the context of inculturation, he spoke to the assembled bishops of the need to move toward a deeper understanding of the mystery of Christ:

> There is no question of adulterating the word of God or of emptying the cross of its power (cf. 1 Cor 1:17) but rather of bringing Christ into the very center of African life and of lifting up all African life to Christ. Thus not only is Christianity relevant to Africa, but Christ, in the members of his body, is himself African.[6]

The church as the communion of saints. A traditional doctrine of the church that makes eminent sense in the Nigerian context is that of the communion of saints. It is part of the creed, though often overlooked. We believe in the communion of the three churches—the church triumphant in heaven, the church militant on earth, and the church suffering in purgatory. Catholicism holds up outstanding men and women as saints, to be venerated and imitated. Above all we look to Mary, queen of all the saints.[7]

In accord with the traditional theological principle that "grace builds on nature," we can find a perfect instance of "nature" in the traditional cultural and religious emphasis of Nigerians on respect for ancestors. A strong sense of solidarity exists in Nigeria between the living and the dead. Parents and grandparents who led good lives and died well are honored and remembered, and their presence is felt in the family, in the lives of those who remain behind. They protect the living and mediate to them the power and love of God. Is not this precisely at the heart of Catholic belief in the communion of saints and in the veneration of saints? We celebrate All Saints Day and All Souls Day on November 1 and 2. Is not this occasion the natural opening to dialogue and correlation with the traditional value of solidarity between living and dead? On the occasion of baptism could not the presence of these ancestors be recognized as part of the prayer of the litany of the saints? In the blessing of homes, should not reference be made to those who have gone before—praying for their eternal rest and recalling the good example, the good lives they have left for us to follow? So, too, burial rites could well incorporate the beautiful sense of solidarity between living and dead that is so strong in traditional African religion.

Mission of the church. At the heart of the church are two constitutive elements, namely the gathering of the community and the sending forth or outward mission of the community. In Nigeria with its rapidly growing church membership, a large part of the energy of the community is devoted to the gathering aspect. This involves catechesis and sacramental preparation and celebration, and is mostly parish-centered. Yet at the same time, if the church is truly to be church, there must be mission to the village, the city, and the nation.

How can Christian values be incarnated first in the lives of Nigerian Christians, and then in and through them in the larger culture and situation? And what particular values or virtues are called for in Nigeria? These are not easy questions to answer, but a theology of inculturation demands that we address them. Here we return to the pastoral circle. An analysis of the Nigerian situation is needed; a reading of the signs of the times, an exposition of values and disvalues, of virtues and vices, must be attempted. After this the church, led by the hierarchy but accompanied with input from the laity, must discuss the response to the situation that is called for, in other words, the more precise nature of the mission of the church in Nigeria. Thus at the local level, the parish should be examining its mission and role in terms of the needs, problems, and opportunities specific to that community. This focus on mission, we need to remind ourselves, is not foreign to the process and goals of inculturation but at its very center. As Jesus Christ became involved in addressing the ills and injustices of his day, as he gave a special care to the poor, the suffering, and the sick, so must the church in this day and age, do likewise in light of the particular situation in which it finds itself.

One particularly excellent example of the attempt to give shape and direction to the mission of the church is the letter from the Nigerian Bishops' Conference, issued in 1972, and entitled "The Church and Nigerian Social Problems." The authors of this letter saw clearly the challenge ahead and the close connection between church mission and inculturation. Let me quote extensively from the end of the letter:

Are we, the Christian community, doing everything
in our power to fight injustices of any kind which
are perpetrated against the dignity of the human
person? Are we preaching the social message of the
gospel, the good news of God's liberation of all
mankind from servility? The seed that we sow, our
message, is the message of the gospel. The soil is
the African, Nigerian soil. The harvest will be a
specific African Christian harvest with its own
unique flavoring preserving the substance of the
character and soul of Africa. . . . Are we trying to
build on all that is best in the African cultural
background, the African communal spirit, the respect for family leadership, the strong human
bonds of extended family relationships?[8]

The thrust of this letter agrees strongly with the thrust of a
theology of liberation, as we will see in a subsequent chapter.

Eucharistic liturgy. The church, as we indicated, involves
both gathering and sending. In the previous section we addressed briefly the mission, or sending. Here we will look at
one aspect of the gathering, namely the gathering around
the eucharistic table at mass. This is an obvious area for
contextualization or inculturation, and also a difficult one.
After reviewing aspects of the Zairean liturgy, I will raise
some questions about liturgy in Nigeria. Here, again, I admit
the limitations. A truly inculturated, contextualized liturgy
can only be developed in a community of faith, in the local
situation. My suggestions are simply ideas, background, and
viewpoints that should be brought to bear on the discussion
and actual process of inculturation.

The aspects of the Zairean liturgy presented here are
not intended for slavish imitation, but rather as a stimulus to

the more difficult process of working toward a Nigerian liturgy. The long process by which the Zairean rite was developed must be gone through in Nigeria. Otherwise it would simply be another case of importation rather than true inculturation.[9]

Music for the Zairean rite draws on traditional African modes rather than European modes, and involves participation by all with voice, gesture, and occasional processions. In addition to hymns sung at the normal times, there is frequently a sung dialogue between the presider and the people. Prayer often takes the form of short acclamations by the presider, and short sung or spoken responses by the entire congregation. This echoes a form of prayer close to the traditional litanies, with constant active responses by the people.[10] In addition to vestments that reflect traditional celebrations, rich symbols of water, fire, and incense are used to heighten the visible, vivid sense of the holy. In the prayers not only are the saints invoked, but also the ancestors who led holy lives; we ask them to be with us. The preparation of the gifts at the offertory includes a procession with dance. The rite of reconciliation, part of every mass, is heightened in the Zairean liturgy, coming after the homily and concluding with the sprinkling of holy water. Throughout the celebration, gestures of prayer, repentance, joy, and community are made, gestures arising from the culture. It is important, too, to realize that the mass is not celebrated exactly the same way in all parishes but allows and calls for flexibility and creativity—all intended to let the people, in the best way possible, express the eucharistic faith that is in them.

How can this process of inculturating the eucharistic liturgy be undertaken in Nigeria. Expertise in liturgical theology is presupposed, expertise that is shared with the leaders of the local community. Another important ingredient would be thorough knowledge of present church regulations on liturgy, and especially the creativity and flexibility that is allowed and encouraged. Also required are immersion in and acquaintance with the various ways in which the local community gathers and celebrates, and knowledge of the traditional ways of praying, singing, and expressing one's faith. Then comes the creative imagining, the long discussion between priest, people, and bishop, the supervised process of experimentation, and the education and catechizing of the larger parish community so that responsible creativity can be shared and tested.[11]

Baptism. How can the Christian celebration of baptism, in particular infant baptism, be creatively adapted so that it will be more expressive of the Nigerian context? Here again, I will offer a few suggestions. Some of these suggestions could be implemented quickly in light of the present flexibility allowed in the baptismal ceremony; others would involve more substantial changes. The naming of the child is most important, and this aspect of the ceremony could be heightened. The reason for the choice of the child's name—possibly one name from the African language, and one from a saint of the Christian tradition—could be given by the parents. Close relatives such as grandparents should be present, and those who are deceased should also be referred to, in order to make them present in spirit. This reference could occur at the beginning of the ceremony, the gathering for the baptism, or it might be part of the invocation of the saints. In accord with the African appreciation of life and of the goodness of creation, the emphasis would fall not so much on original sin (which is nevertheless recalled) as on the love of God who gives life, the wonder of life, the gift of the child to the family and the community.

Baptism by immersion, actually the preferred form according to recent church teaching, might be practiced to illustrate the act of dying and rising with Christ, plunging into the waters of death and rising to new life with Jesus Christ and the community. As mentioned above, more than two hundred of the three hundred and sixty-eight adults baptized at the 1988 Easter vigil at a parish church in Benin City, Nigeria elected baptism by immersion. A large tank was set up in the front of the church with a ladder attached to the outside. The catechumens entered the water wearing old clothing, were immersed, and emerged soaking wet. Then they proceeded to the sacristy where they put on white clothing.

Healing. In Nigeria an enormous amount of work is done by the church in the area of health care through the establishment and administration of hospitals and health clinics. In addition, there is the more directly spiritual ministry to the sick. Yet the sacrament of the anointing of the sick has much unused potential in Nigeria. Catechesis is needed to show that it is no longer the sacrament of the dying, but the sacrament of the sick. And the new rite of the sacrament allows for communal anointing of the sick. Thus the elderly and sick could be gathered regularly in a parish for a powerful, faithful celebration of God's healing love. Although there are healing centers, and individual priests and laity involved in the healing ministry, so much more could be done to enable all Christians to experience the healing power of God.

Many of the independent churches of Nigeria emphasize the healing ministry, and that is one reason for their success. Several centers for healing directed by Catholic priests are now operative, and the enormous response to them is noteworthy. They are in fact places of prayer and pilgrimage for thousands of Nigerians. This phenomenon points again to the need for the church to develop its healing ministry.[12]

So much more remains to be said and done. The area of marriage is a particularly difficult one for the Roman Catholic parish. The very concept and meaning of God could receive new insight from the pervasive religiosity of the African soul. New ways of organizing parish structures and parish teams, more in accord with Nigerian modes of leadership, should be considered. All of these areas call for reflection at the local, diocesan, and national levels.[13] The local parish community must truly try to live the gospel. Then at the diocesan level planning and leadership must be exercised. At the national level, centers are needed to conduct research and experimentation. As a matter of fact, there is such an institute in Nigeria, the Catholic Institute of West Africa, at Port Harcourt. Its mission includes facilitating the incarnation of the Christian gospel on West African soil.

7. Liberation Theology and Inculturation

This situation of pervasive extreme poverty takes on very concrete faces in real life. In these faces we ought to recognize the suffering features of Christ the Lord, who questions and challenges us. They include:

• the faces of young children, struck down by poverty before they are born, their chance for self-development blocked by irreparable mental and physical deficiencies . . .

• the faces of young people, who are disoriented because they cannot find their place in society . . .

• the faces of laborers who frequently are ill-paid and who have difficulty in organizing themselves and defending their rights;

• the faces of the underemployed and the unemployed, who are dismissed because of the harsh exigencies of economic crises . . .

• the faces of old people . . . who are frequently marginalized in a progress-oriented society that totally disregards people not engaged in production.[1]

This powerful statement of the Latin American bishops, issued at Puebla, Mexico, in 1979, provides a concrete framework for the present chapter. In response to the prevalence of poverty and injustice in Latin America, a strong new theology, the theology of liberation, has emerged there. It is an excellent example of a local theology that offers new possibilities, challenges, and hopes not only to those situations in which it is formulated and lived, but also to the universal church. In my estimation it demonstrates beautifully how a theology can emerge from a local context and then in dialogue with the larger church become a leaven, a source of renewal for all theology and all churches.

What does this have to do with inculturation? Inculturation, we have argued, must be a constant of all theology and ministry, whether in the rain forests or Sahara Desert of Africa, or amid the skyscrapers and slums of New York or Rio. In many ways inculturation is most visible in a traditional culture such as Africa. But the church in Latin America is a powerful paradigm of a church coming to grips with its own particular context and culture. Many Christian communities throughout Latin America have done precisely what we are searching for and encouraging in this handbook. They have set the gospel and the Christian tradition over against their contemporary political, religious, and social situation. Their reflection has moved them to confirm the good in the culture and the church, and then to eradicate the evil in the culture and the church. In this way both culture and church approach more closely the vision of the kingdom.

In this chapter, therefore, we will examine how the theology of liberation came to be, what its method and major thrusts are, and how it offers a challenging model of great significance for the inculturation of the gospel in all contexts. For this last point we will rely on the recent Roman documents that have critically examined the theology of liberation.

The Situation of Latin America

To understand adequately the history of the theology of liberation, we must refer to the early history of Christianity in Latin America: how the Christian faith arrived there, how it was associated with the political, colonial powers, how it interacted with the indigenous religions, how the development of the local clergy was postponed, and how nations so often rich in their cultural heritage and natural resources became poor. Latin America is, of course, composed of many nations with varied histories. Yet in general we can speak of a dominant and oppressive colonization process. The result today, as the quotation at the beginning of this chapter depicts, is a situation in which there is a large gap between rich and poor (and most are poor), and where the poor do not have adequate housing, health care, schooling, or attention to basic needs. There is also a gap between the gospel and the local culture or situation. Despite the achievement of some degree of political independence, economic dependence has remained and has increased, as we see from the huge foreign debt currently owed to first world nations by so many Latin American nations.[2]

1962–1965: Second Vatican Council

According to the vision of Pope John XXIII, the church was to open the windows to let in fresh air and then take a fresh look at the world. Pope John convoked the Second Vatican Council, and among its documents the one most significant for Latin America was the Pastoral Constitution on the Church in the Modern World. It begins with these famous words:

> The joy and hope, the grief and anguish of the men
> and women of our time, especially of those who are
> poor or afflicted in any way, are the joy and hope,

the grief and anguish of the followers of Christ as well (no. 1).

The church, in accord with its outspoken tradition in the encyclicals on social justice, was to reach out in a special way to the poor, the suffering, the weak, and the marginated. The bishops of Latin America took up this challenge both individually and as a group in CELAM (The General Conference of Latin American Bishops). Someone has described the effect of Vatican II on Latin America as that of a violent earthquake. While a bishop such as Dom Helder Cámara worked among the poor of Brazil, Camilo Torres left the priesthood to join the guerrillas of Colombia and was killed in 1966. Social-studies centers were established to examine the political and social situation. The conviction emerged among many that development—which was supposed to improve the economies of Latin America—was not working. Stronger cries for liberation, for more radical change, began to be heard. In 1967 Pope Paul VI issued his encyclical "On the Development of Peoples." This document, directed most specifically to developing nations such as those in Latin America, clearly encouraged the church in its growing commitment to the elimination of injustices and to the building of a more just society. "Development," a new name for peace, stood at the center of this encyclical.

1968: Medellín

The Second General Conference of Latin American Bishops (CELAM II) was held at Medellín, Colombia, in 1968. In preparation for their discussion, the bishops saw slides and photographs of the conditions afflicting so many of their people—pictures of poverty and hunger, of unemployment and homelessness. The bishops reflected on the fact that the economic development they had sought and had been led to expect was not forthcoming. Conditions were worsening rather than improving. In light of this reality, they began to speak of the need for more radical change, the need for liberation.

In terms of the pastoral circle, the bishops at Medellín carefully examined their cultural situation, the first pole of the circle, and found it to be far from the vision of the kingdom of God. Thus the documents issued by this bishops' conference move from an emphasis on development to a call for liberation: the political and economic theories of development were found wanting; a more radical solution, that of liberation, was needed. One way to approach such a solution was to encourage the establishment of basic Christian communities where reflection on the Bible and Catholic teaching, as well as on local conditions and injustices, would take place. In reflecting on what we see as the third pole of the pastoral circle the bishops realized that the entire church— laity, priests, bishops, and catechists—had to be involved in the transition from the old to the new, in the effort to truly live the gospel. So strong and challenging were the documents issued by this conference that they are rightfully called the Magna Carta of the theology of liberation.[3]

The bishops, though they were leaders in the inception of liberation theology, were not alone. The groundwork had been prepared by Christians at the local level, who in the basic communities had begun to analyze their situations and to articulate liberating Christian responses. Theologians and scripture scholars had also begun to reflect on the radical message of liberation in the Old and New Testaments. This momentum increased after 1968, when conferences and consultations were held to disseminate the documents of

Medellín and to deepen the collective understanding of the biblical and historical roots of liberation.

Post-Medellín

In 1971 Gustavo Gutiérrez, a Peruvian priest, published in Spanish a book that was to become the classic text of liberation theology. It was translated into English two years later as *A Theology of Liberation* and remains a basic source and benchmark for this new direction in theology.[4] During the 1970s the impact of Latin American theology of liberation began to be felt in other areas of the globe.

In 1975, in response to the Roman synod of 1974 on the topic of evangelization, Pope Paul VI issued his encyclical letter "On the Evangelization of Peoples." With this document the language of liberation became enshrined in official papal teaching. To be sure, the pope affirmed that liberation must be integral, that is, not only political and economic, but, above all, offering spiritual liberation from sin and the effects of sin. In a passage that has been cited frequently in subsequent papal writings and speeches, Paul VI wrote:

> The church, as the bishops (of the synod) repeated, has the duty to proclaim the liberation of millions of human beings, many of whom are its own children—the duty of assisting the birth of this liberation, of giving witness to it, of ensuring that it is complete. This is not foreign to evangelization.[5]

The encyclical also made the first official reference to the basic Christian communities and gave guidelines for their growth. It called them a hope for the universal church provided that they keep centered on the word of God, remain attached to the local church, maintain sincere communion with their pastors and the magisterium, and show themselves to be universal in all things and never sectarian.[6]

Here we see a clear example of how the theology of liberation, the strategy of forming basic Christian communities, and the special option of the church for the poor are no longer the sole responsibility of Christians in Latin America, but a challenge to all Christians. A local theology, a theology incarnated in the soil of Latin America, had become a proposal and an opportunity for all Christian churches through the instruction of this papal apostolic exhortation.

In that same year, 1975, a conference was held at Detroit where representative theologians from North and South America discussed the significance of liberation in the North American context. In 1976 in Tanzania and in 1977 in Ghana, conferences assembled theologians from many third world countries to discuss these new directions in theology.[7]

The year 1978 was the year of three popes. Because of the election of Pope John Paul II in that year, the bishops of Latin America postponed the Third General Conference of Latin American Bishops (CELAM III) to the following year. They met then in Puebla, Mexico, with the pope in attendance. While some feared that there might be a withdrawal or pullback from the forward thrust of the theology of liberation, no such withdrawal took place. Rather, the bishops again affirmed and deepened the commitment of Latin American Catholics to the achievement of justice. The strategy of the basic Christian communities and the option for the poor were reaffirmed, as the citation given at the beginning of this chapter attests.[8]

One example of the consequences of this unequivocal theology of peace and justice for all was the assassination of

Archbishop Oscar Romero of San Salvador on March 24, 1980, as he was celebrating mass. Having witnessed the murder of one of his own priests because of a position advocating justice for the poor, Archbishop Romero had begun to speak out strongly against certain policies, and for that he paid with his life. His death was only one of many. Numerous laymen and laywomen, catechists, priests, sisters, and religious were persecuted, imprisoned, tortured, and put to death because they preached and lived the liberating message of the gospel.[9]

In 1984 and 1986 the Roman Congregation for the Doctrine of the Faith issued two documents specifically on liberation theology. The first, entitled "On Certain Aspects of the Theology of Liberation," opens by stating that "the gospel of Jesus Christ is a message of freedom and a force for liberation."[10] While it is somewhat critical of some aspects of liberation theology, since the movement itself is diverse, one has to say overall that it affirms the validity of the church's commitment to work for liberation at all levels. The second, a lengthier and more positive document, "On Christian Freedom and Liberation," affirms and assures that the insights and the basic direction of liberation theology now have a significant role to play in the formulation of all Christian theology for all contexts.[11]

Method and Thrust of Liberation Theology

From this all too brief chronological history of the theology of liberation, I will now highlight some of the key elements and explore their implications for inculturation. Inculturation, as we have seen, demands a special focus on method, a method of theology and ministry that enables the local church to be truly local and truly creative in its particular context. We have described this method in terms of the pastoral circle. Inculturation calls for a set of attitudes, or dispositions, in both individuals and groups as they attempt to theologize for a particular context.

Liberation theology, too, places heavy emphasis on method and calls for a shift from some earlier ways of doing theology. Gutierrez, for example, shows that liberation theology involves not simply reflection on faith—which traditional theology calls for—but praxis. The end product is not simply understanding, but understanding that leads to transformation. With reference to the pastoral or hermeneutical circle, liberation theology spends much time and effort on the examination and analysis of the context, the cultural situation in which the Christian community finds itself, the first pole. In Latin America, the context is all too often a situation of poverty and injustice. Whereas cultural anthropology may be the most useful discipline for examining cultures in the African context, the disciplines of political science and sociology may serve better in Latin America. Certain tools of Marxist analysis have been employed there in the examination of class distinctions and pervasive injustices. We may note that this use of Marxist categories and methods has come under criticism from Rome—not so much for the analysis itself, as for the ideology that stands behind the analysis, namely a tendency toward atheism and an approach that might lead to conflict and violence rather than to peaceful means of achieving social change.[12]

Rather than focusing exclusively on the sins of individuals and the response of charity to alleviate the sufferings of the people, liberation theology analyzes the social and structural conditions that have led to the situations of injustice and poverty. What is needed in addition to charity, and in a sense prior to charity, is justice. In light of this analysis concrete strategies for action and change must be formulated. How and where is this to be done? Here we turn to a key component of the theology of liberation, namely the formation of small or basic Christian communities.[13] The transformation of individuals into active, committed Christians occurs in these groups, and then through their concerted efforts transformation begins to take place in local communities. It is in these base Christian communities that local theology is formulated. Often with the guidance of a trained leader these groups, which are composed mainly of laymen and laywomen, discern how the gospel and the Christian tradition speak to their particular situation. In other words, these communities exemplify very well what transpires in the pastoral or hermeneutical circle that is at the core of the process of inculturation. The pastoral agent, the third pole of the pastoral circle, is viewed in Latin America most correctly not as a lone individual priest or theologian, but as the leadership group or indeed the entire base Christian community reflecting, working, and planning together collaboratively.

When these Latin American communities look to the second pole of the pastoral circle, the Christian message and tradition, one particular theme that continually arises from their reflections is the special love of God for the poor and the marginated. The story of Moses and the powerful message of the prophets confirm their own search for justice and liberation. Jesus Christ in his teaching of the beatitudes, in the parables, and in his own life and actions revealed that the love of God goes out in a special way to the poor and the sick, the sinner and the oppressed. The church in turn, as liberation theology reminds us, is to carry forward this particular emphasis of the teaching and ministry of Jesus.[14]

This special love has been described in recent papal

documents as the "love of preference for the poor." To be sure, it is not exclusive but it does move, as Jesus did, in sympathetic love toward the needy. Yet it goes even deeper. The church is called on not merely to be *for* the poor, that is, reaching out to the poor; it must be a church *among* the poor, and finally, and most challengingly, a church that is reborn *from* the poor.[15]

The model for this theology of liberation with its concern for and insertion among the poor is, of course, Jesus Christ. He who was rich became poor for our sakes. He emptied himself, taking the form of a servant. He came to bring good news to the poor, release to captives. Jesus Christ was the word of God made flesh. In their focus on Jesus Christ, liberation theology and the theology of inculturation are one: Jesus remains the classic model for liberation, and the classic model for inculturation and incarnation.[16]

Impact and Challenge of Liberation Theology

Christianity and Christian theology have always been pluralistic. The New Testament itself presents four gospel portraits of Jesus, and in addition the letters of Paul and the letter to the Hebrews which afford further rich insight into the mystery of Jesus Christ. The history of theology offers us the achievements of a Thomas Aquinas and a Bonaventure in interpreting the mystery of Jesus Christ for their day and age. The perspectives and perceptions of particular theologians and churches that stand the test of time and are in continuity with the gospel then become part of the universal Christian heritage.

Is this not happening today with the theology of liberation? No longer can it be viewed simply as a local theology, a way of inculturating gospel values into Latin America. No longer can we say that the message of liberation, the formation of small Christian communities, and the love of preference for the poor are necessary only for that part of the Christian world. No, as we explore, read, and learn from liberation theology, we see that it touches Christian faith wherever that faith is—and this for the simple but profound reason that liberation theology is based on the gospel. The very title of the recent 1986 Roman document, "Instruction on Christian Freedom and Liberation," indicates that we are now speaking about an ingredient of all Christian theology and Christian life. While occasioned by the growth and tensions within liberation theology in Latin America, this document is addressed to all Christians, to the universal church. And it is exerting an effect on assemblies of national conferences of bishops as well as on local groups of Christians.

Liberation theology is therefore having a deep impact on the universal church. Essays have been written and conferences have been held on the theology of liberation and its implications for every continent. Black theology in North America and in South Africa turns to liberation theology for support and inspiration.[17] Liberation theology is indispensable to the struggle of African nations to be truly free, free to preserve and develop their own rich cultural heritage. Feminist theologians and Hispanic theologians in the United States have learned much from the pain and struggle of the Latin American churches.

How does one learn from liberation theology? Must every local church do exactly what liberation theology tries to do in Latin America? There are no simple answers to these questions, but a few remarks can be made. Instead of slavish imitation, what is called for is attention to the method and attitudes of liberation theology. We do not imitate Jesus

Christ in all the particular details of his life; rather we try to understand the center, the gospel Spirit that empowered and led him. So too with liberation theology: instead of importing it as such to North America or Africa, we try to do in our own context what they have done in theirs. We gather in small groups, analyze the cultural context or situation, and then confront it with the gospel and the Christian tradition in a manner that leads to transformation. Liberation theology, in other words, furnishes us with a concrete example of inculturation and a method for truly inculturating gospel values into our particular situations. The process we described by means of the pastoral circle agrees very well with the process of liberation theology. It demonstrates a way of reflection that will be liberating from sin, sinful structures, and the effects of sin, as well one that will lead to the incarnation or inculturation of positive Christian gospel values in a particular context.

A final word on this topic comes from Asia, where the impact of liberation theology is being increasingly felt. At a symposium held in Japan in 1985, Aloysius Pieris declared that there can no longer be a theology that is non-liberational; theology is valid only if it originates, develops, and culminates in the process and praxis of liberation. And this, he affirmed, is precisely the implication of the two Roman instructions on liberation. He went on to explain that "the genesis of a liberation theology overlaps with the genesis of an authentically local church."[18] If a local church is immersed and involved in the struggles of its people, then a truly local theology and a theology of liberation can emerge. His conclusion states precisely the point of the present chapter: "This is why we insist that inculturation and liberation, rightly understood, are two names for the same process!"[19]

The challenge of liberation continues in its place of origin, in Latin America. Now it has been taken up by the churches of Asia, Africa, and North America. The shape and form of liberation may vary, in light of the differing faces of injustice and deprivation, but the church in any culture can no longer be blind or deaf to the call for authentic, integral liberation. Inculturation of gospel values in each and every situation inescapably involves the imperative of liberation.

8. Inculturation in a Modernized Society

In Chapter 5 we noted that inculturation must take place wherever Christian ministry is practiced. After examining how inculturation proceeds in a more traditional society such as Nigeria, and the paradigm of inculturation provided by the church in Latin America with its mission of liberation, we turn now to a modernized society, in this case the United States.[1]

To speak of inculturation in the United States may seem surprising or shocking, since Americans often think of themselves as living in a Christian culture. Yet more and more we are seeing that this is not true, that non-Christian and anti-Christian values are very much at work in our culture. In many sectors of American society there is a resistance to gospel values, so much so that some speak of the United States as a neo-pagan society or culture![2] In recent years there has been talk of Europe becoming again the object of Christian mission; I believe we can say the same about the United States. In fact, I would go so far as to say that the most important mission and challenge for the American churches today, far more important than the dialogue among different Christian denominations and the dialogue with atheism, and even more important than the dialogue with traditional cultures, is the mission of the churches to the modernized society in the United States.

Why is this mission so important? First, because what happens in the United States is likely to have significant effects on developing nations. The technology invented or standardized in the United States is, for better or worse, the

110

envy and goal of many peoples of the world. There is a rush toward modernization, a rush that often bypasses awareness of the ambiguities and dangers of modernization, and thinks only of its apparent advantages. A second reason why this mission is important is that the modern western culture is proving resistant to the gospel. As Lesslie Newbigin explains, in many areas of Asia, Africa, and Oceania, the church is growing steadily or even spectacularly. But in areas dominated by western culture, the church has leveled off or is shrinking, and the gospel appears to be falling on deaf ears.

How can we describe or identify modern American culture? I suggest two approaches. First, try to imagine the United States as it was eighty years ago, and think of how things have changed. Recall the advances in technology, the birth of the computer, access to world communications via television and satellite, new methods of farming, airplane and space travel, the emerging world of bio-engineering, nuclear power and nuclear threats, the size and influence of transnational corporations. All of these changes point in different ways to the creation of a new world that is now taken for granted, a world quite different from the more rural, simplified life of the nineteenth century.

Some would define modernization as the increasing proportion of inanimate as opposed to animate sources of power. Instead of human strength or animal power, we use electrical, mechanical, or nuclear power to move mountains and to build cities. Modernization surely means greater control over our environment, the proliferation of technological ways of thinking, and the growing use of mechanical power to assist the human brain and body. The new world of the computer and word processor seems to advance almost every day.

A second approach to understanding modernity and modernized culture would be to travel to a developing nation and observe life in a remote village. There one would find no electricity, no running water, dirt roads with no cars, few if any modern conveniences, no bank, no supermarket, and little communication with the world beyond the village. These external differences between a village in a developing nation and a major city in the United States point to more profound personal, societal, and psychological differences. Modernized cultures have undergone profound qualitative and quantitative changes in the political, economic, social, ecological, and cultural spheres.

While mission and inculturation have been primarily applied by bringing the gospel to traditional non-Christian cultures, they are also at work in the effort of the church to be truly Christian in a modernized culture or society like the United States.

Pastoral Circle Applied to the USA

Building on the chapter on method, we will now inquire in a preliminary way into how the pastoral circle helps in the process of inculturation of gospel values in the United States. The first step is to examine the situation or culture. Here I would emphasize the need to see and feel the ambiguity of the modernized world. Unless we are convinced that it is terribly ambiguous, that is, a mixture of positive and negative elements, we will be swept up uncritically by its negative as well as its positive elements. By ambiguity, I do not mean vagueness or cloudiness. Rather, I mean the more literal sense of the word, namely, that things have two sides to them—in this case a positive and a negative side. The theologian Paul Tillich spoke eloquently of the ambiguity of all human culture and achievement: "He who is not aware of the ambiguity of his perfection as a person and in his work is not yet mature; and a nation which is not aware of the ambiguity of its greatness also lacks maturity."[3] This sense of ambiguity ensures a critical attitude toward modernization. It calls us to discern and foster the good, constructive elements of modernization, and to fight against the harmful, destructive elements.

The ambiguity of modernization is exemplified by such observations as the following: increased mobility allows us to expand our horizons, but it also brings rootlessness; automation eases the physical work load, but it can also turn us into automatons; the very high standard of living in the United States is achieved to some extent at the expense of third world peoples; while we send astronauts into space, the number of starving people on earth increases; television with all of its potential can too easily become a one-eyed monster preventing family members from talking to each other; expenditures for nuclear swords far surpass expenditures for the plowshares that will yield food, education, and health care; excessive use of energy may result in exhaustion of natural resources. Each of these facets of modern culture demands further exploration and critical awareness on the part of individuals as well as groups. Along with many other aspects of modernized societies they call for a Christian response and for the efforts of Christians to inculturate gospel values into modern culture.

One way to begin that process is to reflect on the vices that are apparent in such a society, and then to envision the virtues that are needed to counteract those vices. Vices reflect negative, destructive elements, and virtues reflect constructive elements. Vices indicate what is opposed to the will of God and to gospel values; although they originate in individuals, vices also infect social structures and organizations.

Thus vices and virtues must be examined on both individual and societal levels. In the following paragraphs three specifically modern vices will be highlighted, and then three corresponding virtues. In highlighting these virtues and vices we are in fact moving toward the pole of the Christian message in the pastoral circle. We are beginning to make a Christian evaluation of and response to the ambiguities of modern culture. We might note the similar practice of Latin American liberation theology, which takes as an important starting point reflection on the vices or injustices present in its culture.

Vices

Failure to transcend one's limited perspective in both time and space. In modern society we have the possibility of knowing and communicating with peoples far distant from us. We have more accurate predictive powers concerning future trends. But this makes even more culpable our all too common view of myself, my family, my city, my nation, as the center. We fail to take into account the needs of the world community and the needs of future generations. Ultimately this narrow vision is an expression of sin as selfishness. It can be linked with the failure to believe in the Christian God as the God of all persons in all places and times. We refashion God into our own narrow, household or national, and present-centered, god.

Passivity before and complicity with complex systems. Again self-centered, we prefer to avoid the difficult task of informing ourselves and accepting responsibility for our actions. We use the excuse of ignorance and blame evil results on the complexity of the system. By this passivity, this handing over of personal responsibility for our actions, we allow impersonal forces, technological and physical power solutions, to take priority over solutions based on personal relationships and social justice. In fear we refuse to accept the responsibility for the Christian belief that we are our brothers' and sisters' keepers.

Consumerism, concupiscence, and curiosity. I take these three words to be roughly synonymous, indicating an attitude that makes us want to draw the whole world into ourselves. It involves a desire for abundance, for quantity rather than quality, a fascination with the novel, an unsatisfiable greed, a grasping for the bigger and seemingly better. We measure our success by our possessions; luxuries become "necessities" while so much of the world lacks the real necessities of life.

Pope John Paul II criticized this attitude in his encyclical *Sollicitudo Rei Socialis,* in which he spoke of the dangers of superdevelopment:

> This superdevelopment, which consists in an *excessive* availability of every kind of material goods for the benefit of certain social groups, easily makes people slaves of "possession" and of immediate gratification, with no other horizon than the multiplication or continual replacement of the things already owned with others still better. This is the so-called civilization of "consumption" or "consumerism," which involves so much "throwing-away" and "waste" (no. 28).

He continues with strong words directed against the crass materialism that has resulted from blind submission to sheer consumerism!

Virtues

Virtues are our graced attempts to incarnate the attitude of God into the human situation, here specified as the situation or context of modernized culture. As Christians, we turn to aspects of the life, death, and resurrection of Jesus Christ that help to illuminate our lives. Taking the Christ event as my point of departure, I will suggest three virtues to counteract the vices that have just been described.

Enlarging one's sympathies toward global awareness and responsibility. In contrast to self-centeredness is self-transcendence, the ability to look beyond or to transcend one's narrow interests in space and time. Self-transcendence means stewardship for the future rather than exploitation of the earth's resources to serve present needs and greeds. A broadened range of sympathy involves sensing that the joys and sufferings of those who live at a distance are finally inseparable from our own joys and sufferings. This wider loyalty corresponds to an enlarged and more adequate view of God as the God of all persons, male and female, and as the God who especially hears the cry of the poor. God can no longer be simply the god of myself, my family, my community, my nation; such a god is ultimately an idol or false god, one made according to my narrow and limited image and perspective.

The words concerning the enlargement of one's perspective relate most closely to the theme of human solidarity as frequently reiterated by Pope John Paul II, most recently in the encyclical cited above on social justice. Solidarity, he writes, is

> not a feeling of vague compassion or shallow distress at the misfortunes of so many people, both near and far. On the contrary it is a *firm and perse-*

vering determination to commit oneself to the common good; that is to say, to the good of all and of each individual, because we are *all* really responsible *for all* (no. 38).

Wisdom as the integrative understanding that leads to responsible action. In light of the increased specialization caused by modernization, and the corresponding alienation and fragmentation in the personal and social spheres, there is a greater need for wisdom. Wisdom here means the ability to see connections, to integrate the various elements of modernized society into some unified vision, and then to relate that vision to God as the ultimate source and truth of reality. The wise person constantly asks *why*, until the partial explanations come together into a coherent whole. This vision of the whole leads to action based on one's hierarchy of values, which will take into account the needs, aspirations, and rights of all humankind.

Simplification of life style. In contrast to the consumerist mentality, conversion to a life style of simplicity, frugality, or even austerity becomes necessary if humanity is to hand on the good gifts of the earth to future generations. To put it bluntly, the earth can sustain our needs but not our greeds. A simple life style would give priority to personal values and interpersonal relationships over material possessions and relationships based on physical power. Such simplification of life style is one concrete way in which the preferential but non-exclusive option for the poor—so well set forth in liberation theology—could be practiced in a modern culture.

This preliminary naming of vices in a modernized society and the virtues needed to counteract them is one way to indicate how gospel values might begin to become incarnate in modern culture. At bottom, it is an attempt to enflesh the values and life pattern of Jesus Christ into this age, with

Jesus' vision of God as the Father of all people, and Jesus' faithful struggle against the religious and political forces of his day. The living of these virtues would be our response to take up the challenge of the Pastoral Constitution on the Church in the Modern World, as we accept our responsibility to be citizens of a modernized society.

The incarnation of gospel values in a modernized culture, can only be done by a mature, faith-filled, educated Christian laity. The laity are already inserted in the marketplace, in educational, business, banking, and governmental institutions, and it is here that gospel values will make a difference. Clergy and bishops have their role, too, as teachers of the faith and in encouraging and empowering the laity in their most difficult task. The formation of small groups of Christians who gather to discuss these issues, along the lines of the basic Christian community model of church, would seem to be a firm step in the right direction.

Examples of Inculturation

I will conclude this chapter with several examples of efforts to inculturate gospel values into a modern culture such as the United States. Two of the most recent pastoral letters of the American bishops address crucial issues: "The Challenge of Peace: God's Promise and Our Response," and "Economic Justice for All: Catholic Social Teaching and the U.S. Economy." These two letters can be viewed as attempts to employ the pastoral circle to examine the issues of peace and economic justice and to bring Christian gospel values to bear on these issues. The letter on the economy, we might note, could not have been written without the input, insight, and challenge that came to the United States church from Latin American liberation theology. It is to the laity in business and educational institutions, in the military and in government, that the bishops turn to carry out this process of inculturation.

Other examples of attempts at contextualization or inculturation are the many other varied letters of the United States bishops or groups of bishops that address more particular questions and areas such as the Hispanic peoples, black Catholics, the issue of the land in Appalachia or the middle west, and the native American population.[4] Most recently, the draft of the pastoral letter on women, "Partners in the Mystery of Redemption," furthers the dialogue on ways in which women play essential roles in inculturating gospel values into American society through their personal witness and ministry.[5] Washington, D.C. is the locus for a number of agencies and institutes involved in reflecting on the church in the United States. Among them would be the Center for Concern, the Woodstock Center, and the Quixote Center. Each of them in its own way fosters the dialogue between American culture and the gospel.

In New York City, not far from each other, are two institutional examples of the beginnings of inculturation. At the heart of the financial center of the United States, and indeed the world, is the Wall Street Jesuit Office. Here business leaders meet to talk and pray with their colleagues and competitors, with the aid of resource personnel, in a setting organized and led by Jesuit priests. A few miles away is another Jesuit apostolate, the Nativity Mission Center. Here grammar school students, mostly Hispanic, are tutored so that they will be able to finish grammar school and gain entrance into good secondary schools. Both the Wall Street Jesuit Office and the Nativity Mission Center illustrate many dimensions of the process of inculturation. In both places, Christian gospel values are being discussed and inculturated into different sectors of American society.

The challenge is immense. And because of the impact of a modernized culture such as the United States on the world's future, it is a challenge that will affect not only the church in the United States but the world church. Yet as the theory of inculturation reminds us, all inculturation is a two-way street. If the church in the United States is to be truly Catholic, Christian, Roman, and American, then it must learn from the world church. The insights of Latin America on the role of the church in the work for justice, the insights of the African church on the nature of celebration and on the healing power of the church, and the insights of the Asian church on the mystery and transcendence of God must become part of the consciousness of the American church. If inculturation is taken seriously, then every church, including the American church, is both a learning and a teaching church. But as inculturation reminds us, priority must be given to listening and learning. This is a lesson that the church in the United States sometimes finds very difficult to accept.[6]

9. Conclusion

A handbook on inculturation remains only that—a book, a tool, that can assist in the process. The handbook itself is not inculturation. Yet it serves a valuable function if it encourages, enlightens, and leads one into the process of inculturation. As we have seen, actual inculturation is not easy. It demands a set of attitudes, a method, painstaking research, and the cooperative effort of a group. It may well call for conversion from previous attitudes concerning the church's mission and ministry. Much easier would be the simple transplantation of the gospel from one culture to another. It would again be easier as well as un-Christian to allow the culture to dominate and replace Christian values, which could happen in the United States. Both of these courses of action would be self-defeating, though. And as liberation theology demonstrates, obstacles and opposition will arise as one tries to do something new, to creatively inculturate gospel values into a particular situation or to challenge prevailing cultural values that may be un-Christian.

To move into the new and unknown is risky, but this is not sufficient reason to make us timid. Christian faith demands courage, the courage of the gospel, the courage of Jesus Christ as he made his way even to Jerusalem. Whereas imposition or translation or adaptation may have seemed adequate models for the mission of the church in another era, what is needed now is the courage to undertake true and radical inculturation. Examples of the latter are beginning to emerge, but an uncharted future lies ahead. The way forward demands deep faith in the power of the gospel and in the rich tradition of the church. It calls equally for faith in the presence of God already at work in new cultures and contexts. Saint Paul's image in Romans 8, that of the groaning of all creation and the expectation of new life, is inseparable from true inculturation.

Several themes stand out as we look back over this handbook on the meaning and method of inculturation. One overarching idea is the need for insertion. The leaders of the church, the ministers and the theologians, must be inserted in, involved with, and committed to the concrete lives of those they serve. At the same time, leaders must be familiar with and immersed in scripture and the Christian tradition. Then the Spirit who spoke through the prophets and who speaks through the tradition is heard again today, the same Spirit who is already present in the lives of the people. The people themselves are encouraged to be Christian as the Spirit guides them in their particular situations.

We must also see that inculturation is something ongoing and natural, something that is taken for granted in good Christian ministry. It is not something artificial or something done in the classroom, library, or laboratory. Rather, it is the ongoing way of being Christian wherever one finds oneself. Although at present inculturation is required as a special, separate discipline or approach to theology and ministry, this is the case only because we have failed to practice inculturation in the past and must therefore correct previous inadequate methods of theology and ministry. What inculturation means, in a word, is being fully and truly Christian in a particular, cultural context or situation.

Next, one turns to the importance of the Christian community itself in the process of inculturation. It is not the work of the pastoral agent or priest, even if he or she is most significant in inaugurating the process. As we saw in the chapter on inculturation in the United States, it is only through the laity who are involved and inserted that gospel values can be inculturated. Again as we saw in the chapter on method, the pastoral agent or the theologian must be viewed as a coordinator, a facilitator of the group. Inculturation is carried out by the group. In other words, every Christian must be involved in inculturation if it is to be effective; this is so for the simple reason that every Christian is gifted, graced, and inspired by the Spirit to be Christian in light of the circumstances of his or her life, in private and in public, in the home and in the community.

Finally, we repeat again the need to listen. Inculturation is more listening than teaching or speaking. It is an act of faith—and faith always involves listening—in the saving will and presence of God offered to all men and women. Eventually one speaks, one engages in dialogue as one tries to inculturate gospel values into a particular situation, but first and foremost one must listen.

In this vision of the church, a church from below, a church truly inculturated into the multiform cultures around the world, we have the basis for a truly catholic church. While retaining ties with the larger church, and for Catholics this means the Roman church, the local churches will show forth to the larger church their own particular ways of living and sharing the gospel of Jesus Christ. Specific gifts and talents, specific insights into scripture, will not be stifled or submerged, but rather allowed to flourish and grow; they will be available to the larger church for its edification. The catholicity and the universality that we seek still lies ahead of us. The local churches have their indispensable part to play in contributing to this catholicity.

Notes

Introduction

1. See "Economic Justice for All: Catholic Social Teaching and the U.S. Economy," in *Origins,* 27 November 1986; "The Challenge of Peace: God's Promise and Our Response," United States Catholic Conference, 1983; "The Hispanic Presence: Challenge and Commitment," *Origins,* 19 January 1984.

2. For a recent comprehensive examination of the meaning of the catholicity of the church, see Avery Dulles, *The Catholicity of the Church* (Oxford: Clarendon Press, 1985).

3. Pope John Paul II, "The African Bishops' Challenge," an address to the bishops of Kenya given on 7 May 1980. It is found in *Origins,* 28 May 1980, p. 29.

4. Perhaps the closest to what we are attempting is the most helpful volume of Robert Schreiter, *Constructing Local Theologies* (Maryknoll, N.Y.: Orbis Books, 1985). I am heavily indebted to this work. My own handbook functions more on the introductory level, and also varies considerably from the scope of his work. Two examples of works in which we see inculturation in process—books that could be read together with this handbook—are Vincent Donovan, *Christianity Rediscovered* (Maryknoll, N.Y.: Orbis Books, 1985) and Eric de Rosny, *Healers in the Night* (Maryknoll, N.Y.: Orbis Books, 1985). These would clearly exemplify what might be called radical inculturation, resulting from deep immersion in the life and culture of Africa.

The collection of essays entitled *Inculturation: Its Meaning and Urgency* (Nairobi, Kenya: St. Paul Publications, 1986), by J.M. Waliggo et al., touches on many of the topics treated here, but lacks the overall order and comprehensiveness of this study. *African Ecclesial Review* 22 (December 1980) is entirely devoted to inculturation and is a rich resource, but it does not function as an introductory handbook. *One Faith, Many Cultures,* ed. Ruy O.

Costa (Maryknoll, N.Y.: Orbis Books, 1988) contains the presentations of a conference on inculturation, indigenization, and contextualization, held in Boston in 1986. It is wide-ranging in the
topics, traditions, and cultures it treats, and shows the complexity
of the issues that inculturation must deal with.

As this manuscript was being prepared for publication, an
important book of Alyward Shorter appeared, entitled *Towards a
Theology of Inculturation* (Maryknoll, N.Y.: Orbis Books, 1988). He
brings a wealth of knowledge and experience to his treatment of
inculturation. While much of it overlaps with this presentation, my
handbook has a specific chapter on method, and another chapter
on inculturation in a modern society such as the USA. In addition,
I suggest a number of concrete areas of church life in Nigeria
where inculturation is called for.

5. See Pedro Arrupe, "Letter to the Whole Society on Inculturation," in *Studies in the International Apostolate of Jesuits,* 7 (June
1978): 9.

Chapter 1

1. Arrupe, "Letter to the Whole Society," 2.
2. The study of how men and women differ in ways of thinking
and feeling is in its infancy. See, for example, Mary Belenky et al.,
Women's Ways of Knowing: The Development of Self, Voice, and Mind
(New York: Basic Books, 1986), and Carol Gilligan, *In A Different
Voice: Psychological Theory and Women's Development* (Cambridge,
Mass.: Harvard University Press, 1982).
3. Pope John Paul II, "The African Bishops' Challenge," 29.
4. See Karl Rahner, "A Basic Theological Interpretation of
the Second Vatican Council," *Theological Investigations* 20 (New
York: Crossroad, 1981): 77–89.
5. Peter Sarpong, "African Religion and Catholic Worship," a
talk given to the Eucharistic Congress in Philadelphia, in August
1976. Cited in A.O. Erhueh, *Vatican II: Image of God in Man*
(Rome: Urbaniana University Press, 1987), 298–99.
6. Aloysius Pieris, in *Mission in Dialogue,* ed. Mary Motte and

Joseph R. Lang (Maryknoll, N.Y.: Orbis Books, 1982), 429–32, emphasizes that inculturation should be natural and ongoing. Rather than being a separate goal, it should result from ongoing immersion in the lives, struggles, and culture of a particular community. Another brief essay that makes this same point very well is by Regis B. Ging, M.M. "How Can Inculturation Take Place? Via a Complex, But Natural, Process," in *Mission Forum,* Japan Region, Series 13, Nos. 3 & 4, 1984, pp. 18–20. In chapter four of this book we will focus on the agent of inculturation, and emphasize that the agent should work collaboratively with the community, at least with the leaders of the local community.

Chapter 2

1. For further explanation and elucidation of the various terms, Schreiter's *Constructing Local Theologies* is very useful, as well as two essays by Ary A. Roest-Crollius: "What Is So New about Inculturation?" *Gregorianum* 59 (1978): 721–38, and "Inculturation and the Meaning of Culture," *Gregorianum* 61 (1980): 253–74.

2. Pope Paul VI, "Evangelization in the Modern World," no. 63. This apostolic exhortation is of crucial importance in giving guidelines for the process of inculturation. It shows the connections between evangelization and inculturation, and how each of them gives a direction to the mission of the church.

3. Pope Paul VI in his address at the closing of the All-African Bishops' Conference, given at Kampala, Uganda, July 31, 1969. This groundbreaking address can be found in *Acta Apostolicae Sedis* 61 (1969): 573–78.

4. Alyward Shorter, *African Christian Theology* (Maryknoll, N.Y.: Orbis Books, 1977), 150.

5. For a fuller account of this new strategy, see Shorter, *African Christian Theology,* 150–55.

6. In addition to Schreiter, see the essay of Shoki Coe, "Con-

textualization as the Way toward Reform," in *Asian Christian Theology*, ed. D.J. Elwood (Philadelphia: Westminster, 1980), 48–55.

7. Samuel Rayan, "Flesh of India's Flesh," *Jeevadhara* 33 (May–June 1976): 260.

8. Arrupe, "Letter to the Whole Society," 13.

9. Pope John Paul II, as reported in *L'Osservatore Romano*, 24 February, 1982.

10. Don Browning, *The Moral Context of Pastoral Care* (Philadelphia: Westminster, 1983), 73. Schreiter and Roest-Crollius also discuss the various understandings of culture. This discussion of the proper understanding of culture uncovers a wealth of resources and opinions. Rather than enter deeply into that discussion I have given a general, but comprehensive description of culture.

Further significant input on the meaning of culture and its significance for Christian theology can be gained from a study of chapter two of *Gaudium et Spes*, the Pastoral Constitution on the Church in the Modern World. While not strictly defining culture, it describes what culture refers to and the various elements that come together to make up a given culture. One might say that the theme of this book, inculturation, is precisely the effort of theologians and pastoral agents to come to grips with the challenge set before the Christian churches in this important chapter of that key document of the Second Vatican Council.

11. Archbishop D.S. Lourdusamy, "On Theological Formation," *Vidyajyoti* (October 1979): 400.

12. See *Ad Gentes*, nos. 6 and 22, among other places, where we read that the "seeds of the Word" are present in many cultures. This is echoed in Paul VI, *Evangelii Nuntiandi*, no. 53.

13. The imagery of planting seeds, and nurturing plants and trees, occurs frequently in the letters and addresses of Pope Pius XII concerning the missions. See, for example, *Evangelii Praecones* (1951).

14. This image was developed beautifully and powerfully in an address by Robert Rush given at the 1977 Jesuit Mission Dinner in New York City. It is printed in *The Jesuit* (Spring 1978).

Chapter 3

1. For a basic one volume history of the missions, see Stephen Neill, *A History of Christian Missions* (New York: Penguin, 1984). Although Neill does not focus on inculturation, much of what he describes could be seen as various attempts at inculturation throughout the history of the church.

2. The Council of Jerusalem is treated inter alia in *The Jerome Biblical Commentary,* under the "Life of Paul"; *Peter in the New Testament,* ed. Raymond Brown, Karl Donfried, and John Reumann (New York: Paulist, 1973) 43–48; Avery Dulles, "An Ecclesial Model for Theological Reflection: The Council of Jerusalem," in James Hug, *Tracing the Spirit* (New York: Paulist, 1983), pp. 218–41; Paul J. Achtemeier, *The Quest for Unity in the New Testament Church* (Philadelphia: Fortress, 1987).

3. Gregory the Great, "Letter to Abbot Mellitus," in J. Neuner and J. Dupuis, eds., *The Christian Faith,* rev. ed. (New York: Alba House, 1982), no. 1102.

4. Speech of Archbishop Helder Cámara at Rockefeller Chapel, November 1974. It is reported in the *National Catholic Reporter,* 17 September 1976.

5. Pope Nicholas V in his bull *Dum Diversas,* issued in 1452.

6. Ricci to General Acquaviva, 1592, *Memory Palace* by Jonathan Spence (New York: Viking, 1984), 115. This volume also contains further material on Ricci. A very readable account of Ricci is found in *Wise Man from the West* by Vincent Cronin (New York: Dutton, 1955). See also George Minamiki, *The Chinese Rites Controversy* (Chicago: Loyola University Press, 1985), and George Dunne, *A Generation of Giants* (Notre Dame, Ind.: University of Notre Dame Press, 1962). The entire issue of *Lumen Vitae* 40 (1985) is devoted to China and the heritage of Ricci.

7. In *The Christian Faith,* no. 1109; this citation is often referred to in the history of missiology. For further readings on Roberto de Nobili, see Vincent Cronin, *A Pearl to India* (New York: Dutton, 1959), and Francis X. Clooney, "Christ as the Divine Guru in the Theology of Roberto de Nobili," in *One Faith, Many Cultures,* ed. Ruy Costa, 25–40.

8. See his apostolic letter *Maximum Illud,* in *The Christian Faith,* no. 1112. Many of these key papal documents on the missions, including some recent addresses of Paul VI and John Paul II in Africa, are found in *Modern Missionary Documents and Africa,* ed. Raymond Hickey (Dublin: Dominican Publications, 1982). The introduction to this volume traces the development of the modern missionary movement in Africa as it is reflected in papal documents.

9. This is found in his encyclical *Rerum Ecclesiae* of 1926, in *The Christian Faith,* no. 1117.

10. See his letter referred to above, *Evangelii Praecones,* in *The Christian Faith,* no. 1128.

11. Several essays in a recent volume on Vatican II explore the implications of Vatican II for mission and inculturation. See *Vatican II: The Unfinished Agenda,* ed. Lucien Richard (New York: Paulist, 1987), especially for Richard's essay entitled "Mission and Inculturation: The Church in the World."

12. Pope Paul VI, address at the closing of the All-African Bishops' Symposium. For a collection of official church teachings and texts since Vatican II, see *The Church and Culture Since Vatican II,* ed. Joseph Gremillion (Notre Dame, Ind.: University of Notre Dame Press, 1985).

13. Pope Paul VI, address at the closing of the All-African Bishops' Symposium.

14. Pope John Paul II, "The African Bishops' Challenge," no. 6.

15. See its message to the people of God, final report, D.4. This is found in *The Extraordinary Synod. 1985* (Boston: St. Paul's Editions, 1986).

Chapter 4

1. See, for example, *Ad Gentes,* nos. 6 and 22.

2. For an introduction to Rahner's theology, see *A World of Grace,* ed. Leo J. O'Donovan (New York: Crossroad, 1981). Rahner's views on grace, revelation, and the anonymous Christian

offer, it seems to me, a solid foundation for a theology of inculturation.

3. An essay that relates views of Jesus Christ to positions in ecclesiology is Peter Schineller's "Christ and Church: A Spectrum of Views," in *Theological Studies* 37 (December 1976): 545–66.

4. *Gaudium et Spes,* no. 58.

5. We will examine more carefully the significance of the basic Christian communities for inculturation in the chapter on liberation theology.

6. An excellent essay that puts mission at the center of the church and relates it to inculturation is Roger Haight's "The Established Church as Mission: The Relation of the Church to the Modern World," in *The Jurist* 39 (1979): 4–39.

7. A number of Catholic theologians have begun to reflect on the specifically Catholic nature of the Roman Catholic tradition. Among them are David Tracy, *The Analogical Imagination* (New York: Crossroad, 1981), especially chapter 10, Lawrence S. Cunningham, *The Catholic Experience* (New York: Crossroad, 1986), and Rosemary Haughton, *The Catholic Thing* (Springfield, Ill.: Templegate, 1979).

8. Juan Luis Segundo, *The Liberation of Theology* (Maryknoll, N.Y.: Orbis Books, 1976), 77–81, and "On a Missionary Awareness of One's Own Culture," in *Studies in the International Apostolate of Jesuits* (September 1974): 33–47.

9. Catalina Arevelo, in an unpublished paper at a conference on the mission of Jesuits today.

10. For a thorough discussion of the meaning and importance of the conciliar statement on the hierarchy of truths, see William Henn, "The Hierarchy of Truths Twenty Years Later," *Theological Studies,* 48 (September 1987): 439–71.

11. Rahner studies this question in his essay "Reflections on the Problems Involved in Devising a Short Formula of the Faith," in *Theological Investigations,* vol. 11 (New York: Seabury, 1974), 230–44. He has an earlier essay in vol. 9 of *Theological Investigations,* and he presents an example of the short formula in a talk given at the Concilium conference of 1970. This is found in *The Catholic Mind* (December 1970): 24–27. In the same issue are

found similar short summaries of the faith by Raymond Brown and Hans Küng. The epilogue of Rahner's *Foundations of Christian Faith* (New York: Seabury, 1978) consists of reflections on the need for a short formula and then examples of three creedal statements.

12. Rahner, *America,* March 10, 1979, 180.

Chapter 5

1. Several sources come to mind as helpful for this discussion of method in ministry. James D. Whitehead and Evelyn Eaton Whitehead, in *Method in Ministry* (New York: Seabury, 1981), present their method for theological reflection and Christian ministry using the image of a triangle rather than a circle. Schreiter's *Constructing Local Theologies* shows the complexity of the interrelationships between gospel, church, and culture in his second chapter, "Mapping a Local Theology," Juan Luis Segundo offers his version of the hermeneutical circle, with a heavy emphasis on being self-critical and on reflection as leading to praxis, in *The Liberation of Theology.* This chapter is an adaptation and expansion of my essay "A Method for Christian Ministry," in *Emmanuel* 87 (March 1981): 137–44.

2. See Paul Tillich, *Systematic Theology I* (Chicago: University of Chicago Press, 1963), 59–66.

3. The field of anthropology is vast. Clifford Geertz, Marvin Harris, Ward Hunt Goodenough, Victor Turner, and Mary Douglas are among the anthropologists who have been helpful to theologians. On this topic, see "Theology and Anthropology: Time for Dialogue," by G. Arbuckle, in *Theological Studies* 47 (September, 1986): 428–47. See also Marcello de Carvalho Azevedo's *Inculturation and the Challenges of Modernity* (Rome: Gregorian University, 1982). His dialogue with anthropologists and his bibliography are worth noting. On the general topic of social analysis, see J. Holland and Peter Henriot, *Social Analysis* (Maryknoll, N.Y.: Orbis Books, 1983).

4. On the theme of collaboration as essential to all ministry

and church life see, for example, *Collaborative Ministry* (Notre Dame, Ind.: Ave Maria Press, 1987), by Loughlan Sofield and Carroll Juliano.

5. The letter of Pedro Arrupe on inculturation, referred to above, outlines various attitudes and virtues needed for successful inculturation. He links these with the Ignatian tradition of discernment and docility to the inspiration of the Holy Spirit.

Chapter 6

1. The literature on theology in the African context is growing rapidly. I will indicate here some of the books that I have found most helpful for understanding the process of inculturation in Africa, and in Nigeria in particular. The writings of Walbert Bühlmann are a good introduction. His earlier book, *The Coming of the Third Church* (Maryknoll, N.Y.: Orbis, 1978), alerted the universal church to the tremendous growth of Christianity and Catholicism in Africa. His more recent book, *The Church of the Future* (Maryknoll, N.Y.: Orbis Books, 1986), describes the exciting developments taking place in Latin America, Africa, and Asia. Two volumes that connect closely with the writings of Bühlmann are Deane William Ferm's *Third World Liberation Theologies: An Introductory Survey* and *Third World Liberation Theologies: A Reader*. Both were published by Orbis Books in 1986. Ferm presents brief introductions to and excerpts from theologians of Latin America, Asia, and Africa. For the history of Christianity in West Africa, see Lamin Sanneh, *West African Christianity* (Maryknoll, N.Y.: Orbis Books, 1983). Three introductory texts on African theology are Aylward Shorter's *African Christian Theology,* John S. Pobee's *Towards an African Theology* (Nashville, Tenn.: Abingdon, 1979), and Gwinyai H. Muzorewa's *The Origins and Development of African Theology* (Maryknoll, N.Y.: Orbis Books, 1985). An essay that provides an overview of various theological directions in Africa is Justin S. Ukpong's "Current Theology: The Emergence of African Theologies," in *Theological Studies* 45 (September 1984): 501–36.

African Theology en Route (Maryknoll, N.Y.: Orbis Books, 1979), edited by Kofi Appiah-Kubi and Sergio Torres, is a useful collection of theological essays by African authors. Particularly insightful into the culture of Africa is Joseph G. Donders' *Non-Bourgeois Theology* (Maryknoll, N.Y.: Orbis Books, 1985). An African woman theologian, Mercy Amba Oduyoye, presents her theological reflections on Christianity in Africa in *Hearing and Knowing* (Maryknoll, N.Y.: Orbis Books, 1985). Inculturation as the writing and living of a fifth gospel is set forth by Joseph G. Healey in *A Fifth Gospel* (Maryknoll, N.Y.: Orbis Books, 1981).

2. Schreiter explores and gives examples of such texts in chapter 3 ("The Study of Culture") of his *Constructing Local Theologies.*

3. For an important and comprehensive reflection on catechesis, see the apostolic exhortation of Pope John Paul II, "On Catechesis in Our Time," which was issued in 1979 and develops themes from the synod of bishops held in 1977 on the theme of catechesis. In no. 53 the pope relates catechesis to inculturation. He states that although the term inculturation may be a neologism, "it expresses very well one factor of the great mystery of the incarnation." He adds, "We can say of catechesis, as well as of evangelization in general, that it is called to bring the power of the gospel into the very heart of culture and cultures." More recent discussions on the desirability and feasibility of a universal catechism, and its implications for the process of inculturation, are now in process.

4. See his "Apostolic Letter on First Tonsure, Minor Orders and the Subdiaconate" (*Ministeria Quaedam*), where he suggests these possibilities. This document can be found in *Vatican II, The Conciliar and Post Conciliar Documents*, ed. Austin Flannery, vol. 1 (Collegeville, Minn. Liturgical Press, 1984) 427–32.

5. The essays that have been written thus far mostly indicate one or other line of development for an African christology; no comprehensive work has yet emerged. An excellent summary of many of these themes is found in "African Christology," *Theological Studies* 48 (September 1987): 505–15, by Raymond Moloney.

The significance of Jesus Christ as healer is developed in *Jesus and the Witchdoctor* (Maryknoll, N.Y.: Orbis Books, 1985), by Aylward Shorter.

6. Pope John Paul II, "The African Bishops' Challenge."

7. See, for example, E.W. Fashole-Luke, "Ancestor Veneration and the Communion of Saints," in *New Testament Christianity for Africa and the World*, ed. M.E. Glasswell and E.W. Fashole-Luke (London: S.P.C.K., 1974), 209–21.

8. "The Church and Nigerian Social Problems," a letter issued by the Catholic Secretariat of the Nigerian Bishops' Conference (Lagos, Nigeria, February 1972). In this letter we clearly see an example of African interaction with the theology of liberation as set forth in Latin America.

9. For further descriptions of the Zaire rite liturgy, see E. Elochuckwu Uzukwu, *Liturgy, Truly Christian, Truly African*, Spearhead, no. 74 (Eldoret, Kenya: Gaba Publications, 1982), 59–66.

10. The way Africans pray in their traditional religions is, of course, a great resource, and one that needs to be studied in the process of inculturation. See Alyward Shorter, *African Christian Spirituality* (London: Chapman, 1978), and his essay "Divine Call and Human Response: Prayer in the Religious Traditions of Africa," in *The Way* 23 (January 1983): 65–76.

11. An overview of liturgical adaptation can be found in *Cultural Adaptation of the Liturgy* by Anscar J. Chupungco (New York: Paulist, 1982). More specifically in regard to Africa, see the work of Uzukwu referred to above, and *Living Worship in Africa Today*, ed. Brian Hearne, Spearhead no. 62 (Eldoret, Kenya: Gaba Publications, 1980).

12. In addition to Shorter's *Jesus and the Witchdoctor,* referred to above, see Michael C. Kirwen, *The Missionary and the Diviner* (Maryknoll, N.Y.: Orbis Books, 1987), and E. Milingo, *The World in Between* (Maryknoll, N.Y.: Orbis Books, 1984). Archbishop Milingo was archbishop of Lusaka, Zambia, and involved in Christian healing. He was then reassigned to a Vatican office, the Pontifical Commission on Migration, Refugees, and Tourism. He continues his healing ministry in Italy. See also *Anointing and Healing in*

Africa by Jac Hetsen and Raphael Wanjohi, Spearhead no. 71 (Eldoret, Kenya: Gaba Publications, 1982).

13. A book that explores alternative ways of ensuring an adequate supply of ordained ministers is Raymond Hickey's *Case for an Auxiliary Priesthood* (Maryknoll, N.Y.: Orbis Books, 1982). He would like to see mature catechists, married or single, ordained as auxiliary priests to supplement celibate priests trained in the more traditional seminaries. On Christian marriage in Africa—a major problem—see Eugene Hillman, *Polygamy Reconsidered* (Maryknoll, N.Y.: Orbis Books, 1975). In addition to numerous essays that have appeared in *African Ecclesial Review* on this topic, see also Benezet Bujo, "Polygamy in Africa: a Pastoral Approach," *Theology Digest* 32 (Fall 1985). A letter of 25 March 1988 from the Secretariat for Non-Christians (published in *L'Osservatore Romano*, 2 May 1988) encourages pastoral attention to and dialogue with African traditional religion. A wide range of themes from Catholic theology, most of which have been mentioned in this chapter, can be enriched and deepened through this dialogue, according to the letter.

Chapter 7

1. "The Puebla Final Document," in *Puebla and Beyond*, ed. John Eagleson and Philip Scharper (Maryknoll, N.Y.: Orbis Books, 1979) 128–29.

2. For a history of Latin America and of liberation theology, see Enrique Dussel, *A History of the Church in Latin America: Colonialism to Liberation (1492–1979)* (Grand Rapids, Mich.: Eerdmans, 1981). A brief overview of and introduction to liberation theology can be found in Phillip Berryman's *Liberation Theology* (Oak Park, Ill.: Meyer, Stone Books, 1987). See also *The Praxis of Suffering* by Rebecca S. Chopp (Maryknoll, N.Y.: Orbis Books, 1986), especially 1–27. For a description of recent events in Latin America and the involvement of the USA in those events, see Penny Lernoux's *Cry of the People* (Garden City, N.Y.: Doubleday, 1980).

3. For the documents of Medellín, see *The Church in the Pres-*

ent-Day Transformation of Latin America in the Light of the Council, 2 vols. (Washington, D.C.: United States Catholic Conference, Division for Latin America, 1973).

4. Gustavo Gutiérrez, *A Theology of Liberation* (Maryknoll, N.Y.: Orbis Books, 1973). A new and slightly revised edition of this work with a new introduction by Gutiérrez was published by Orbis Books in 1988.

5. Pope Paul VI, *Evangelii Nuntiandi,* no. 30.

6. Ibid., no. 58.

7. See *Theology in the Americas,* ed. Sergio Torres and John Eagleson (Maryknoll, N.Y.: Orbis Books, 1976), for the 1975 Detroit conference; *African Theology en Route,* ed. Kofi Appiah-Kubi and Sergio Torres (Maryknoll, N.Y.: Orbis Books, 1979), for the 1977 conference held in Accra, Ghana, and *Irruption of the Third World,* ed. Virginia Fabella and Sergio Torres (Maryknoll, N.Y.: Orbis Books, 1983), for the conference held in New Delhi, India in 1981. At each of these conferences there was a rich and challenging interchange among theologians from Asia, Africa, Latin America, and North America. A fine example of the universal applicability of the theology of liberation is found in the work of Roger Haight, *An Alternative Vision: An Interpretation of Liberation Theology* (New York: Paulist, 1985). Through dialogue with liberation theologians on the major areas of Christian theology, he shows that wherever theology is done and lived it must be liberating.

8. See *Puebla and Beyond* for the documents of the Puebla conference of bishops, in addition to introductory and background material.

9. For the writings of Oscar Romero, see *Voice of the Voiceless* (Maryknoll, N.Y.: Orbis Books, 1985), a collection of some of his pastoral letters and sermons. One particularly powerful and comprehensive essay by Romero is "The Political Dimension of Christian Love," published in *Commonweal,* March 26, 1982, 169–72. For his life, see *Archbishop Romero: Martyr of Salvador* by Placido Erdozain (Maryknoll, N.Y.: Orbis Books, 1981). See also two books by James R. Brockman on Romero: *The World Remains: A Life of Oscar Romero* (Marynoll, N.Y.: Orbis Books, 1982) and a selection

of Romero's writings edited by Brockman, *The Violence of Love* (San Francisco: Harper and Row, 1988).

10. *Instruction on Certain Aspects of the Theology of Liberation* (Boston: St. Paul's Editions, 1984) 3.

11. *Instruction on Christian Freedom and Liberation* (Boston: St. Paul's Editions, 1986). As the introduction states, this document is concerned with Christian doctrine on freedom and liberation. Although it arose because of the dialogue with liberation theology as set forth in Latin America, it now affirms that freedom and liberation belong to the traditional patrimony of the churches. Showing how this teaching is based on the Old and New Testaments and on tradition, it then outlines the liberating mission of the church in chapter 4 and subsequent chapters. In no. 96 it explicitly relates liberation to the challenge of inculturation. "Inculturation," the document states, "is not simply an outward adaptation; it is an intimate transformation of authentic cultural values by their integration into Christianity. . . ." Then the document asserts that "the church wishes to devote all her energies to this task, so as to evoke an immense liberating effort."

12. For a clear study of the encounter between Marxism and Christianity, see Arthur F. McGovern, *Marxism: An American Christian Perspective* (Maryknoll, N.Y.: Orbis Books, 1980).

13. The literature on the base Christian communities is enormous and growing. Particularly helpful is *The Challenge of Basic Christian Communities,* ed. Sergio Torres and John Eagleson (Maryknoll, N.Y.: Orbis Books, 1981). See also two books by Leonardo Boff, *Ecclesiogenesis: The Base Communities Reinvent the Church* (Maryknoll, N.Y.: Orbis Books, 1986), and *Church: Charism and Power* (New York: Crossroad, 1986). The BCCs of Latin America have had a great impact on the church of Africa, where a similar phenomenon is referred to as the small Christian community (SCC). For an example of this, and for a more extended bibliography on the SCC in Africa, see *From Outstations to Small Christian Communities,* by Patrick A. Kalilombe, Spearhead nos. 82–83 (Eldoret, Kenya: Gaba Publications, 1984). *Aspects of Christian Community Building in Africa,* Spearhead no. 75, by Jac Hetsen and James Holmes-Siedle (Eldoret, Kenya, Gaba Publications,

1983), is another example of the cross-fertilization between Latin American and African ideas of church as community. Not only in Africa, but in India too, the BCC model of church has been introduced and regarded as crucial for inculturation. See Joseph Prasad Pinto's excellent and comprehensive study of the Indian phenomenon, *Inculturation Through Basic Communities: An Indian Perspective* (Bangalore: Asian Trading Corporation, 1985). A recent volume which incorporates much of the previous literature on the base Christian communities is by Marcello de Carvalho Azevedo, entitled *Basic Ecclesial Communities in Brazil: The Challenge of a New Way of Being Church* (Washington, D.C.: Georgetown University Press, 1987).

14. The option for the poor is now a commonplace in recent papal teachings, for example the encyclical *Sollicitudo Rei Socialis*. Donal Dorr, in his book *Option for the Poor: A Hundred Years of Vatican Social Teaching* (Maryknoll, N.Y.: Orbis Books, 1983), shows the development of this theme as a challenge to the universal church. For a Latin American treatment, see Gustavo Gutiérrez, *The Power of the Poor in History* (Maryknoll, N.Y.: Orbis Books, 1983).

15. On this insertion among and identification with the poor, see especially Jon Sobrino, *The True Church and the Poor* (Maryknoll, N.Y.: Orbis Books, 1984), 84–124.

16. Sobrino has written two books on christology in the context of liberation theology: *Christology at the Crossroads* (Maryknoll, N.Y.: Orbis Books, 1978), and *Jesus Christ in Latin America* (Maryknoll, N.Y.: Orbis Books, 1987). See also the book of essays edited by Jose Miguez Bonino, *Faces of Jesus: Latin American Christologies* (Maryknoll, N.Y.: Orbis Books, 1984).

17. One example of this is *The Kairos Document: Challenge to the Church* (Grand Rapids, Mich.: Eerdmans, 1986), which is a theological comment on the political crisis in South Africa. Pope John Paul II during his visit to Africa in 1985 emphasized the links between inculturation and liberation. See his powerful address in the Cameroons, "The Cry for Authentic Liberation," published in *Origins* 15 (29 August 1985). He calls for a liberation that is fully Christian and fully African and adds that a tireless effort at incul-

turation must be pursued if the faith is not to remain on the surface (no. 8). For the impact of liberation theology on black theology in the United States, see the various writings of James Cone, and the book edited by Cone and Gayraud Wilmore, entitled *Black Theology: A Documentary History* (Maryknoll, N.Y.: Orbis Books, 1979). Another volume that discusses the impact of liberation theology in Africa is Laurence Magesa's *Liberation Theology in Africa,* Spearhead no. 44 (Eldoret, Kenya: Gaba Publications, 1978).

18. Aloysius Pieris, "A Theology of Liberation in Asian Churches?" *The Month* (September 1986): 231. Two collections of essays by Pieris have recently appeared: *An Asian Theology of Liberation* (Marynoll, N.Y.: Orbis Books, 1988), and *Love Meets Wisdom: A Christian Experience of Buddhism* (Marynoll, N.Y.: Orbis Books, 1988).

19. Ibid. See also the essay by Pieris "Inculturation in Non-Semitic Asia," in *The Month* (March 1986): 83–87. Once again we see that inculturation and liberation must go together, whether in Latin America, Africa, North America, or Asia.

Chapter 8

1. This chapter is based on a long essay of mine, "Ten Summary Statements on the Meaning, Challenge, and Significance of Inculturation as Applied to the Church and Society of Jesus in the United States, in Light of the Global Processes of Modernization," *Inculturation: Working Papers on Living Faith and Cultures,* 2 (Rome: Pontifical Gregorian University, 1983). The theme of this chapter is also explored by Parker Palmer in *The Company of Strangers* (New York: Crossroad, 1983) (the subtitle of his work is "Christians and the Renewal of America's Public Life"), and by Paul Steidl-Meier, in *Social Justice Ministry* (New York: LeJacq Publishing, 1984). Chapters 9 and 10 of the latter book discuss the church and the marketplace, and the church and communications. John Kavanaugh's *Following Christ in a Consumer Society* (Maryknoll, N.Y.: Orbis Books, 1981), and his essay "Capitalist Culture and Chris-

tian Faith," *The Way,* 25 (July 1985): 175–85, make further contributions.

2. See, for example, Lesslie Newbigin, *Foolishness to the Greeks* (Grand Rapids, Mich.: Eerdmans, 1986), 3. He believes that modern western culture, more than almost any other, is proving resistant to the gospel. Bishop Patrick Kalilombe expresses agreement with Newbigin in an unpublished lecture given at a mission symposium held at Maryknoll in September 1986. See also the challenging essay by Newbigin, "Can the West Be Converted?" in *International Bulletin of Missionary Research* 11 (January 1987): 2–7.

3. From his address "The Ambiguity of Perfection," published in *Time,* May 17, 1963, 69.

4. We see here the importance of national and regional conferences of bishops in dealing with the particular problems that their regions must face. Two examples of attempts at inculturation by bishops of a particular region are "Strangers and Guests: A Regional Catholic Bishops' Statement on Land Issues" published in *Origins,* 26 (June 1980), and "This Land Is Home to Me," a pastoral letter on powerlessness in Appalachia by the Catholic bishops of the region, issued in 1975.

5. The draft of this letter appeared in *Origins* 17 (21 April 1988). The subtitle of the draft reads, "A Pastoral Response to Women's Concerns for Church and Society."

6. The letter of the United States bishops on world mission, entitled "To the Ends of the Earth" and published in *Origins* 16 (4 December 1986), makes the point repeatedly that the church in the United States should learn from returning missionaries, and be enriched by their experience and by the faith of Christians around the world (no. 74). It also affirms that the mission of the church in the United States (or anywhere) is inseparable from the challenge of inculturation and liberation. In fact, many of the themes of this handbook are found in the letter.

A long quotation from John Taylor shows the possibilities of and the need for this reverse mission, whereby the first world learns from the third world. In his book *Primal Vision* (London: SCM Press, 1963) he writes:

The question is rather, whether in Buganda and elsewhere in Africa, the Church will be enabled by God's grace to discover a new synthesis between a saving Gospel and a total, unbroken unity of society. For there are many who feel that the spiritual sickness of the West, which reveals itself in the divorce of the sacred from the secular, of the cerebral from the instinctive, and in the loneliness and homelessness of individualism, may be healed through a recovery of the wisdom which Africa has not yet thrown away. The world Church awaits something new out of Africa. The Church in Buganda and in many other parts of the continent, by obedient response to God's calling, for all its sinfulness and bewilderment, may yet become the agent through whom the Holy Spirit will teach his people everywhere how to be in Christ without ceasing to be involved in mankind (p. 108).